Front Cover

left
Alan Morton
Bill Struth   centre
Jim Baxter   Ally McCoist
David Murray
Walter Smith

right
George Young
Scot Symon
Willie Waddell
John Greig
Richard Gough

The Now You Know column in the *Evening Times* is arguably the longest-running sports item in British newspapers.

Fans write in on all manner of sporting topics, not least on matters concerning Glasgow Rangers FC. Over many years columnist and widely respected sports commentator, Bob Crampsey has tried to answer queries and give the facts about the affairs, past and present, of this great club.

NOW YOU KNOW *ABOUT* . . . **RANGERS** is a compilation of the major points of correspondence and a selection of nearly 200 questions that have occupied the minds of letter-writers.

An invaluable treasure trove of information on the proud traditions of Rangers.

now you know *about* . . .

R A N G E R S

Bob Crampsey

© Bob Crampsey & *Evening Times* 1994

Published
Argyll Publishing
Glendaruel
Argyll PA22 3AE
in association with
Evening Times
195 Albion Street
Glasgow G1 1QP

British Library Cataloguing-in-Publication Data.
A catalogue record for this book is available from the
British Library.
ISBN 1 874640 11 4

Typeset and origination
Cordfall Ltd, 041 332 4640

Printing
HarperCollins, Glasgow

Contents

Seventy Years and More of Now You Know

The Now You Know column in the *Evening Times* is almost
certainly the longest-running sports column in Britain. It has been
going since the mid-1920s at least and possibly before that and
for many years was in the hands of the redoubtable Jimmy
McCormack (Jaymak) who spared no individual or sporting body
in his passion for the correct answer.

To read the answers to past correspondents is to sit in on the
industrial history of a vanished West of Scotland. The great and
overwhelming tradition of the column is that correspondents use
noms-de-plume rather than their own names. There was a time
when the column was awash with letters from such as Caulker,
Riveter's Mate, Yarrow's, Hoover Hand, N. B. Loco Springburn,
Pit Deputy and now all such are gone as if they had never been.

The letters themselves are fascinating, ranging from notes
scribbled on crumpled paper with a blunt pencil to elegantly
presented daisy-wheel compositions on headed notepaper.

Naturally fans want to read of their great successes and tend
to skip over defeats and disasters. That does not mean these last
go unrecorded – in an Old Firm situation the "other side" will
always anxiously seek out such knowledge. What the questions
do is firmly indicate those players who have established a special
place in the heart of the support. As the questions come in over

the years the whole story of Scottish football unfolds, the advent of floodlighting, the introduction of competitive European football, the influx in recent years of English and foreign players.

Good times produce more questions than bad. The one time in my recollection when Rangers questions did not form the bulk of my postbag was towards the end of the long period of Jock Stein's domination in the early 1970s.

Certain topics continue to fascinate. Did A ever play in the same side as B? Amazingly often, given that I know there was a 10 year age difference at least, the answer is yes. Many people claim to have been on Rangers' books, so many that if all were true the Rangers staff would have looked more like a census roll than a register of signed players. The great bulk of such claims are spurious and made in the claimant's cups but just occasionally one goes to the team sheet and behold, Teethy McGurk or whoever he is, has had his hour of glory.

Few things are new under the sun. Rangers had foreign and coloured players half a century before popular opinion might credit it.

My commitment in the column is to Scottish football in general of course and this inevitably means that in every club there are a few people whose knowledge of their own single club is greater than mine. This does not matter greatly. When mistakes occur I have been touched and humbled by the almost invariable courtesy with which my correspondents draw attention to errors or omissions.

What opinion have I formed then of the outstanding ambitions of Rangers fans? They want to win the European Cup which would put them up sides with Celtic. They want to win the League Championship ten times in a row which would put them ahead of Celtic. And they want to record seven goals in an official game to avenge the League Cup Final defeat of 1957.

It is sometimes said that footballers command nationwide attention for a few years and are then swept into total oblivion. I am not sure that this is quite true. To this day letters come into the office asking about such players as Dawson, Young and

Woodburn, none of whom has kicked a ball for Rangers in the last 40 years yet they have clearly burned a place into the hearts of everyone who ever saw them in their prime.

No one can understand the industrial West of Scotland who does not understand Association Football. For much of the century that league football has existed Rangers have been predominant in Scotland. Their joys and sorrows have affected a large portion of the Scottish workforce every Monday morning.

My hope is that the answers contained in this book will entertain and inform. In the case of those who are old enough it may revive memories of the Bovril stand at Ibrox, the Govan Burgh band marching sedately round the track, the early kick-offs in the grey winter days before floodlighting and the constant firefly flickering of a thousand cigarettes being lit somewhere in the crowd. And for those so young that they have grown up with the lightweight strips, try to imagine the heavy woollen jerseys that became seven or eight pounds heavier as they were soaked in the rain, try to imagine shin guards that made legs appear like tree-trunks and high heavy boots that in the immortal words of Hugh McIlvanney "chafed you under the armpits". Those pre-tranny days, when the news of what happened elsewhere was gleaned from the weird semaphore of the scoreboard, were for many their introduction to what is still, at its best, the greatest game of all.

A word of caution is due here about the answers. Inevitably some of the answers which were correct at the time of being written have been overtaken by subsequent events. Wherever possible I have tried to indicate the date at which such answers were originally given but this is the only form of editing that has taken place.

Finally, not being at all a fan of those videos where the opposing team never gets over the halfway line, far less scores a goal, I have included a modest proportion of answers on matches where victory on that day did not crown the brow. An account of total unrelieved success is not only boring but inaccurate. The greatest triumphs are enhanced by previous adversity.

CHAPTER ONE

Winning Medals

In recent years it has become the fashion for young players, berated by their managers, to turn on them occasionally and snarl, "Show us your medals, then!" The jibe is illogical. Being a good player is no guarantee of becoming a good manager and several of the great managers would not have been able to answer the question satisfactorily. Bill Struth had no football medals as a player, Scot Symon very few although he might well have had but for the 1939-45 war. And even Jock Stein had only just enough medals to deflect the question.

Apart from anything else, much depends on when the player was on the staff. It seems incredible that such Ibrox giants as Jimmy Gordon, Arthur Dixon and Tommy Cairns do not have a Scottish Cup medal between them but they do not because their time with Rangers coincided with the long Scottish Cup drought.

On the other hand Dougie Gray is well into double figures with League Championship medals and but for that same war would almost certainly have ended up with something approaching twenty, putting himself comfortably out of sight of any foreseeable rival.

Then again the wartime players won almost every competition in sight but at a time when actual physical medals tended not to be given, replaced instead by the more humdrum Savings Certificates. At a time when players were badly paid, allowing for the fact that Rangers players were better off than anyone else, the medals gained over a career were something to be kept in a case or handed on to the grandchildren with the passage of time. That agreeable custom might well be on the way out now as players realise that medals can fetch quite a considerable sum at auction!

The most coveted medal is of course the European Cup Winners Medal of 1972 and possession of this sets its owners apart at Ibrox. Yet in the early days some very valuable and beautiful medals were struck. The Glasgow Charity Cup medal was always well worth having, as were the ones from the Exhibition Cup in 1902. And it was the ambition of every Rangers player to collect the full pre-war set which was effectively Scottish Cup, Scottish League, Glasgow Cup and Glasgow Charity Cup. To do this was sometimes the work of an entire career but the first eleven players of 1929-30 managed this in the course of the season.

During the two World Wars there was of course opportunity to collect medals of another sort and two of Rangers players were decorated during the second great conflict. The ever-popular Willie Thornton was awarded the Military Medal for gallantry during the invasion of Sicily and Ian McPherson, who was making a name for himself in the reserves, was awarded the Distinguished Flying Cross while serving with the Royal Air Force. He later played in England with Arsenal and Notts County.

The modern footballer is sometimes tagged as mercenary and possessing no great club loyalty but he still sets considerable store on winning medals. They are the proof of his footballing existence and ability and so long as Ibrox appears to be the best place to win them then so long will the job of manager and scouts in attracting outstanding prospects to Rangers remain that much easier.

A final tale to show that realism kept breaking in. During the early 1930s the Rangers players were pleased that a prestigious friendly match against an English club was coming up, less pleased that they would each receive a canteen of cutlery for their efforts. Bob McPhail was landed with the delicate task of conveying their feelings to Bill Struth.

Upstairs Mr Struth listened in well-simulated amazement to Bob McPhail's plea that money would be much more acceptable. "But this is cutlery of the highest quality!" he said. "Maybe so, boss," came the reply, "but it's not a lot of use to you if you cannot afford steak!"

According to legend, Bill Struth for once relented.

MEDALS ON AND OFF THE FIELD

BANTAM (Glasgow) Can you tell me if Willie Thornton, former Rangers player and now assistant manager at Ibrox, won a medal in the last war?

Willie Thornton won the Military Medal for gallantry during the Allied invasion of Sicily in 1943.

BARNS PARK (Ayr) How many medals did Jim Baxter gain during his first spell as a Rangers player?

Confining ourselves to the three major competitions, in five seasons he won three Scottish Cup medals, four League Cup medals and three League Championship medals.

BLUENOSE (Carntyne) When recently you credited Bob McPhail with six Cup medals with Rangers why did you forget that Dougie Gray had also won six?

I did not overlook Gray but the question did not concern him. He in fact won his medals in the same finals as McPhail, namely in 1928, 1930, 1932, 1934, 1935 and 1936.

TRUE BLUE (Glasgow) My argument is that when Rangers won the Scottish Cup in 1928 they were given extra medals for players who did not take part in the final and Tommy Muirhead received one.

That is correct. Tommy Muirhead was one of those who received a medal without playing in the final.

J. G. (Glasgow) Please tell me when Dougie Gray joined Rangers and when he left them. How many championship medals did he win with them and how near is Bob McPhail in that respect?

Dougie Gray joined Rangers from the Aberdeen junior side

Mugiemoss in 1925 and played for Rangers until the end of season 1945-46. He won 11 championship medals. Bob McPhail won 9, a total which Alan Morton also achieved.

KIDDYKAR (Lennoxtown) Did Jimmy Duncanson win a Victory Cup medal in 1946?

Not sure if medals were awarded for this competition, Savings Certificates seem more likely just at the end of the war but Duncanson certainly played in the Victory Cup final when Rangers beat Hibernian 3-1 at Hampden Park on June 15, 1946. In fact he scored two of the Rangers goals, Gillick getting the other as against a solitary Hibernian goal from Johnny Aitkenhead.

QUIZ KING (Glasgow) Can you confirm that Derek Johnstone is the only Rangers player to have won four Scottish Cup medals in four different positions? Has any other player of any club ever done this?

Derek Johnstone won medals at No 5 in 1973, at No 11 in 1976, at No 9 in 1978 and 1981, and at No 4 in 1979. I can't positively say that this is unique but I think it most unlikely that any other player has a similar record.

Chapter two

The Ground:
Where Will We Play?

The career of Rangers as tenant and eventually landlord follows in very close parallel that of Queen's Park, from public park to but-and-ben to very large stadium. In both cases there were moves of only a few hundred yards although it has to be said that Rangers got to their goal of a stadium for the 21st century considerably ahead of their Southside neighbours.

It is interesting to note that both clubs started out on public parks, Rangers on Glasgow Green, Queen's Park in the Recreation Ground. The next step was the move to the corrugated iron-enclosed and tin-hutted private park, first Hampden in the case of Queen's, Burnbank for Rangers. The latter came south of the river to Kinning Park and then along to first Ibrox, a couple of hundreds yards nearer the city than the present ground. At the same time the building of the Cathcart Circle Railway line caused Queen's Park to move across Cathcart Road to Second Hampden which would later become Cathkin Park.

Gradually Ibrox assumed its modern shape. The quaint double-barrelled enclosure roof went sometime after the first great war. The mighty stand which could hold 10,500 people began to take shape. A sad side-effect was the demolition of the attractive little villa-pavilion in the corner. With the destruction of the one at Broomfield this year, only Craven Cottage has a surviving example

Monarch of all I survey – chairman David Murray proudly gazes on the reconstructed Ibrox which is now one of the great European grounds

of the time when football was a more social game.

Between the wars Ibrox could accommodate massive crowds but in unacceptable conditions of safety, and this particular bill was called in with melancholy results in 1971. From then on the stadium has been transformed, a feat all the more astonishing when one considers that during much of the rebuilding it was "business as usual".

The result has been a ground which is the equal of any in Europe and the avoidance of a move to the outskirts which would have at a stroke obliterated 100 years of history. It may be true that football is and indeed has to be a business but it will always forget the sentiment which fuels that business at its peril.

CLUB GROUNDS

GIRNIN' GATES (Drumchapel) Where did Rangers first play and when did they move to their first private ground? Had they any other grounds before the present Ibrox?

Rangers first played in 1873 on the Flesher's Haugh on Glasgow Green. During 1875-76 they spent a season at their first private ground at Burnbank, off Great Western Road and then moved to Kinning Park before opening First Ibrox in 1887, a little to the east of the present ground. The present ground was opened on December 30 1899.

FORM 10 (Glasgow) Whereabouts exactly was Rangers ground on Great Western Road?

The Burnbank Ground was on the opposite side of the present St Mary's Cathedral and a few yards towards the east.

CALLING HARRY R. (Cumbernauld)

W Pow of Paisley writes to say that he remembers the change of name from Ibrox Park to Ibrox Stadium being made around 1938. This seems very probable to me given the opening of the Empire Exhibition at Ibrox by King George VI and Queen Elizabeth in May of that year. My best thanks to Mr Pow.

CHAPTER THREE

Disasters and Accidents

We tend to forget the astonishing pulling power of football in the early days of the century. It is certain that when the first six figure crowd assembled it was the biggest gathering of people ever seen in the one place in Scottish history since no one believes the ballad writers' figures about Bannockburn and there were not 20,000 men altogether on the field of Culloden.

The mixture of such numbers within a fairly primitive ground and a high state of crowd excitement was a potentially lethal cocktail. All over Scotland, on any Saturday, a disaster was waiting to happen. The question was not would it happen, but rather when and where.

Ibrox Park at the 1902 International against England was the answer and the statistics of the dead were grim enough in all conscience. The casualty list numbered 25 dead and almost 600 injured as the flimsy wooden terracing collapsed under the sway of the crowd craning forward, so legend has it, to get a better view of the mazy dribbling of the Scottish winger Bobby Templeton. The following verses do not rank as great poetry but they were printed on the memorial cards of the time and have a certain rough poignancy.

LINES ON THE IBROX DISASTER

Brightly dawned that April morning,
Blue skies bade us haste away
Where the flower of Scottish football
Meant to show their might that day.
East and west from every quarter
Happy hearts come trooping in,
Till the gates of sunny Ibrox
Close on the great crowds within.

Ne'er a thought of pending danger,
All are eager for the fray;
Quip and jest and friendly jostle
While the waiting time away.
Hark! is that a sound of creaking?
Timid ones grow pale with fear;
But the thought is soon forgotten
The contending teams appear.

Free and fast the game is raging,
Scotland's sons are pressing sore;
On the tiptoe of excitement
All expect them soon to score.
Then is heard a mighty uproar,
"God have mercy!" someone cries,
Panic-stricken there's a stampede
Which all human power defies.

High above the seething tumult
What an awful sight is seen,
Only a great gap remaining
Where the cheerful crowd had been.
Down below are dead and dying,
Mangled forms lie all around,
Broken-limbed and bruised and bleeding
Like a shambles is the ground.

Willing hands, their hearts nigh failing,
Go to work with tender care,
Till the long, long list of injured
Of their help receive a share.
Brightly dawned that April morning,
Blackest night has been the close,
Our sympathy is with the suffering,
Rest the dead in sweet repose.

Great efforts were made to ease at least the financial burden of the relatives. Rangers put the Exhibition Cup of 1902 up for competition to raise funds and there was a representative match between the two countries.

The next major accident occurred in September 1931, though only one person lost his life, the outstanding Celtic goalkeeper John Thomson. He was injured in a clash with the Rangers centre-forward Sam English. That the collision was accidental there is no doubt, astonishingly at that early time there is a postcard and even a film of the moment of impact which shows that English was legitimately trying to play the ball. Thomson's death was appallingly sad, for even his opponents willingly spoke of his brilliance. But in truth Sam English was every bit as much a victim of that day for although he continued in the game he was never again the same player. Quite blameless, he remained haunted by the dreadful mischance.

In 1961 there was a grim portent of events to come when two people died on Passage 13 which was of course to be the scene of the great disaster at the January game of 1971. This time the death roll was a numbing 66 and the story circulated at the time that Rangers fans leaving the ground after Celtic had taken a lead with only three minutes to go, had tried to fight their way back up the stairs on hearing the cheer that greeted a last-gasp equaliser from Colin Stein.

All the evidence would deny that this happened. Much more probable was that one or more of the leaving crowd simply stumbled and went down, and anyone who has ever been caught

A moment of tragedy – Celtic goalkeeper John Thomson died in hospital after this save at the feet of the blameless Sam English in a league match at Ibrox in September 1931

up in a crowd like that will know that he has often reflected, "One trip and that is it".

Both teams and boards of directors attended a joint service for the victims and out of the wreckage of Passage 13 came the great programme of rebuilding which would eventually ensure that among British grounds Ibrox would have no superior. Benefit matches were held once again and the young Rangers staff had the harrowing task of attending what seemed to be a never-ending succession of funerals. The disaster was all the more affecting in that there had been no suggestion of crowd misbehaviour. It may be of some consolation to the bereaved families to know now that the deaths of their husbands, sons and brothers led to an infinitely greater concern with crowd safety and has dramatically lessened the chance that there will ever again be a calamity of that scale.

DISASTERS AND ACCIDENTS

GRACE STREET (Glasgow) Could you give me both teams in the Ibrox Disaster game of 1902?

Teams were, SCOTLAND, Doig (Sunderland), N Smith, Drummond (both Rangers), Aitken (Newcastle United), Raisbeck (Liverpool), Robertson (Rangers), Templeton (Aston Villa), Walker (Heart of Midlothian), Brown (Tottenham Hotspur), Livingstone (Celtic), A Smith (Rangers).

ENGLAND, George (Aston Villa), Crompton (Blackburn Rovers), Molyneux (Southampton), Wilkes (Aston Villa), Forman (Nottingham Forest), Honiker (Blackburn Rovers), Hogg (Sunderland), Bloomer (Derby County), Beats (Wolverhampton Wanderers), Settle (Everton), Cox (Liverpool).

WEE CHIC (Glasgow) When did Sam English sign for Rangers and how many games did he play for them before the fatal accident to the Celtic goalkeeper John Thomson?

Sam English joined Rangers from Yoker Athletic in July 1931. He played in seven league games before the match in which

John Thomson met with his fatal accident at Ibrox on September 5 of that year.

ANXIOUS MARIE (Bishopbriggs) Was Colin Stein's first goal for Rangers against Celtic the last-minute equaliser in the Ibrox Disaster game of 1971? Was that his only Old Firm goal?

The goal you mention was his first against Celtic but in September 1971 he scored again at Ibrox in a match which Celtic won 3-2.

J. C. L. (Saltcoats) Can you give the age of Sam English at the time of the accident to John Thomson and say how long he was with Rangers?

Sam English was 21 when he signed for Rangers in July 1931 and he went on to Liverpool at the end of season 1932-33.

LONDONER (Croydon) Which teams were playing when the First Ibrox Disaster occurred? Can you give a typical Rangers team of the time?

The match was an international between Scotland and England. The Rangers team which won the Exhibition Cup in 1902 against Celtic read, Dickie, N Smith, Drummond, Stark, Neil, Gibson, McDougal, Wilkie, Hamilton, Speedie, A Smith .

RANGERS SUPPORTER (Drumoyne) Please give teams, score and scorers in the match played in aid of the Ibrox Disaster Fund of 1971.

A Scotland XI beat an Old Firm Select 2-1 before a crowd of 81,405.

SCOTLAND, Cruikshank (Heart of Midlothian), Hay, Gemmell (both Celtic), Stanton (Hibernian), McKinnon (Rangers), Moncur (Nencastle United), Lorimer (Leeds United), Gemmill (Derby County), Stein (Rangers), O'Hare (Derby County), Cooke (Chelsea).

OLD FIRM Bonetti (Chelsea), Jardine, Greig (both Rangers), Murdoch, McNeill (both Celtic), Smith, Henderson (both Rangers), Hughes (Celtic), Charlton (Manchester United), Johnston (Rangers), Best (Manchester United).

Goal scorers were Gemmill and Lorimer for Scotland and Best for the Select.

SURE (Kelvinside) Did Rangers take part in a match against Everton to raise funds after the First Ibrox Disaster?

Rangers and Everton played at Celtic Park on May 3, 1903 and the proceeds went to the Ibrox Disaster Fund. Rangers won the match 3-2.

ROCKED FAN (Glasgow) Please confirm that an explosion occurred during a Rangers v Motherwell match at Ibrox in the spring of 1974. I think it was a midweek match. Please also give score.

On April 24, 1974, a Wednesday, Rangers beat Motherwell 2-1 at Ibrox. Just before half-time a gas cylinder exploded at the east end of the ground hut there were no reports of damage or casualties.

Opposite
A forward's view of the formidable Terry Butcher, an inspirational defender and a great favourite with supporters

CHAPTER FOUR

The Saxon Invasion

If you look closely enough it has always been possible to find the occasional Englishman at Ibrox throughout the club's history but such players were rarities. Between the wars Arthur Dixon was the club's regular centre-half and later their trainer and George Jenkins, the long-time and uncomplaining deputy to Jerry Dawson, was also English-born but these players were so few as to be scarcely worthy of comment.

The incoming Saxon torrent started to flow with the arrival of Graeme Souness. The players fell into three distinct categories. There were the comparative unknowns such as Colin West, Neil Woods, Chris Vinnicombe and Jimmy Phillips who arrived by stealth and left shortly afterwards though not before having given the occasional useful performance. Then there were the players who were very well-known but who turned out for the Scottish club comparatively infrequently. Dale Gordon, Terry Hurlock, Mel Sterland and above all Trevor Francis would fall into this category. Then finally there were the already-acknowledged stars. To be able to list them from memory would qualify the person who managed it for Mastermind and the following roll-call does not pretend to be exclusive but may serve to give some idea of

Opposite and over
Class tells – both Trevor Francis, in a handful of appearances, and Trevor
Steven as a regular, brought their individual skills with them north of the
border

the enormous contribution which the Sassenachs have made to the Ibrox cause over the past eight years or so.

Chris Woods preceded another English-born goalkeeper, Andy Goram although fortunately for club and country Andy was Scotland-qualified. There was the redoubtable captain Terry Butcher, for whom there was no such thing as a lost cause. There was the consummate artistry of Ray Wilkins and Mark Walters, an artistry which encompassed Trevor Steven also and, for the more discerning spectator, Mark Hateley. Those who think that Hateley is simply a marvellously direct finisher should look at the incisively-angled passes which he delivers when he moves wide. It would be perhaps fair to say that Graham Roberts could fairly be placed in the more combative section but his value as a driver was considerable.

The English brigade provoke a fevered correspondence. There are those who write in saying that Rangers, by big money-buying, have distorted the Scottish League. Such letters are by definition not from Rangers supporters. The latter tend to point out, with perfect truth, that it is better that top-level English players are prepared to come to Scotland rather than still have the reverse route which has bedevilled Scottish football for so long. By the early 1980s it seemed that no Scottish club, not even Rangers, would be able to hang on to its players. One or two readers have even made enquiries, only half-jokingly, as to whether there might not be some way in which Mark Hateley could acquire Scottish nationality. Off the field, what is interesting is that some of the Englishmen have grown very fond of their adopted land. Certainly Mark Hateley has and Terry Butcher paid Scotland the ultimate compliment by returning north after his playing days were over and a managing venture at Sunderland had gone awry.

THE SAXON INVASION

ADELPHI STREET (Glasgow) When Trevor Francis came to Rangers what had been his previous club? In all countries how many league matches had he played up until then?

He came to Rangers from the Italian club Atalanta, having previously played in Italy with Sampdoria. When he became a Rangers player he had already made 465 league appearances in England and Italy and after leaving Rangers he made more than a hundred more league appearances with Queen's Park Rangers and Sheffield Wednesday.

EL TEL (Dalry) Who made the most league appearances for Rangers between Mark Walters, Chris Woods and Terry Butcher?

Chris Woods leads with 173 appearances then comes Terry Butcher with 127 and finally Mark Walters with 106.

BANDSTAND (Kelvingrove) Can you fill me in on the career of Neil Woods who was one of the very early English signings for Rangers in the time of Graeme Souness?

Neil Woods came to Rangers from Doncaster Rovers but played only three matches in the League for the Ibrox club. He then returned south and after short spells with Ipswich Town and Bradford City he played for Grimsby Town for at least three seasons and indeed was still on their books at the beginning of the season which has just finished.

CAP AND GLOVES (King's Park) Up until the beginning of season 1993-94 how many England caps did Chris Woods have? How many did he gain while a Rangers player?

From 1985-93 he had 43 caps in all. Of these 20 were gained while a Rangers player and on six of these occasions he came on as substitute.

TOPPER (Yoker) I say that Terry Hurlock, who was signed by Rangers from Southampton, did not play even 20 league games for Rangers.

You are wrong on two counts. He was signed from Millwall and in fact went to Southampton after leaving Rangers. While

Gary Stevens, maurading on the right wing, gets in a cross despite the intervention of two Perth defenders in a league match with St Johnstone

at Ibrox he had 29 league appearances and scored two goals.
WORK IT OUT (Govanhill) What do Terry Butcher and Ally McCoist have in common besides being Rangers players?

I don't care much for things that are riddles rather than questions but one correct answer would be that they both turned out for Sunderland.

CHAPTER FIVE

European Competition

From time to time the question crops up, or rather the statement is made, that Rangers have outgrown Scottish football. I believe a better statement is that increasingly Rangers will he judged by what they do in Europe. The winning of at least one competition a year at home could almost be assumed, as long as Scottish football has the tail it has and there is no doubt that from the supporters point of view, the visit of Marseilles is a more thrilling prospect than a call from Raith Rovers.

It is the European nights which stick in the memory. The triumphs, a lob by the young Sandy Jardine which defeated the Bayern keeper in the semi-final of the Cup Winners cup in 1972, the nail-biting win against Sparta at the third attempt in 1960, the difference of opinion between Harold Davis and the bespectacled Jurion of Anderlecht, the injury to Jim Baxter in Vienna which effectively ended his great days.

There was of course the ultimate triumph of Barcelona in 1972 when joy in victory was put on hold while the fans wondered what UEFA would do in the wake of the disorders which had punctuated the last stages of the game. Europe has given the players the chance to perform at the highest level and of course it has always been a learning process. Sometimes the learning was painful as against Real Madrid in the Bernabeu Stadium and Eintracht in the semi-finals of 1960. Sometimes it was a triumphant assertion that Rangers could manage the very best in Europe as shown by their defeat of Benfica and years later, a splendid performance in Holland against PSV Eindhoven when Tommy McLean and Bobby Russell combined to score one of the best goals ever seen in Europe from any side.

Any team which in the course of a season beats the English champions home and away and then goes through its league section undefeated in the European Cup, as Rangers did in season 1992/93, has most certainly earned its spurs. It is clear from the letters what the memories are, of Greig driving on his team-mates, of Henderson tearing opposing defences apart by superlative ball control at speed, of Baxter turning on the style almost contemptuously.

In the heat of a European tie there is a marked tendency to see only one side and Ibrox provides no exception. But in the calm light of dawn the bulk of the support would agree that the Continentals had and have much to teach us.

Not least is the European ability to sustain fierce pressure and then to go on the lightning counter-attack, assisted by their ability to play the ball out of defence.

The bit players have also made their contribution. It is a fair guess that Gary McSwegan will do nothing else in his career so dramatic as his goal for Rangers against Marseilles at Ibrox when he had just come off the bench. Increasingly the yardstick to judge a Rangers player will be, "Could he get in to a good European side?"

THE EUROPEAN GAMES

D. SMITH (Cambuslang) I think you will find that the goalkeeper of Sparta Rotterdam wore glasses when playing against Rangers at Ibrox in a European Cup tie.
I have checked this out and the spectacled keeper, Muhring, did not play against Rangers although as you say he did play against Celtic at Parkhead in a friendly match which Celtic

Scot Symon (left) greets Wolves manager Stan Cullis (right) on the occasion of the Cup Winners tie between the two in March 1961. Between them is the match referee J Cesare

*won 5-0. The Sparta goalkeeper in all three Rangers games
was Van Dijk.*

**A. W. W. (Mount Florida) Can you confirm that before Sandy
Jardine settled at right-back he played on a number of occasions
at centre-forward? My friend says he has NEVER played at
centre-forward for Rangers.**

*In his early days Sandy Jardine operated in both the No 8 and
the No 10 spots. He was at No 9 for both legs of the Fairs Cities
Cup tie with Vojvodina in September 1968 when Rangers won
3-0 on aggregate and there were other instances.*

**WEAVERS (Condorrat) Please give the Rangers teams which
met Wolverhampton Wanderers home and away in the late
1950s. I am sure that Doug Baillie was at centre-forward in the
Ibrox match.**

*These matches were played in March and April of 1961 (note
dates). The competition was the Cup Winners' Cup. At Ibrox,
where Rangers won 2-0 their team was, Ritchie, Shearer,
Caldow, Davis, Paterson, Baxter, Scott, Wilson, Baillie, Brand,
Hume. In the return match which was drawn 1-1 the defence
was the same but the forward line read Wilson, McMillan, Scott,
Brand, Hume.*

**BRIDGETON X (Glasgow) Give the Rangers teams in the two
matches against Eintracht Frankfurt in the European Cup semi-
finals in 1960.**

*The following Rangers side lost 6-1 in Germany, Niven, Caldow,
Little, Baird, Paterson, Stevenson, Scott, McMillan, Murray,
Millar, Wilson. In the second leg at Ibrox which Eintracht won
6-3 Davis was at right-half and the forward line read Scott,
McMillan, Millar, Baird, Wilson.*

**WOODHEAD BAR (Hamilton) When Rangers met Leeds
United in the UEFA Cup at Elland Road in the early 1960s was
there closed circuit television at Ibrox and if so what was the
attendance?**

*When Leeds United won this match 2-0 in the second-leg
quarter-final tie on April 9, 1968 (a bit later than you thought)
the game was televised on closed circuit at Ibrox. An incredible*

43,177 attended with prices for admission being £1, 10/- and 5/-.

MARTIN (Glasgow) Please give the Rangers team that got to the final of the Cup Winners Cup in 1967 and name the Bayern Munich scorer

The following Rangers side lost 1-0 to Bayern Munich after extra time at Nuremberg on May 31, 1967, Martin, Johansen, Provan, Jardine, McKinnon, Greig, Henderson, A Smith, Hynd, D Smith, Johnston. The goal was scored by Roth.

R. MEE (Glasgow) Please give me the Rangers goal scorers in the European tournament matches against Tottenham Hotspur. Have Rangers ever won a match home and away against English opposition in a European competition?

Rangers of course defeated Leeds United home and away in the European Cup in season 1992-93. They also took three points out of four against Wolves back in 1961. In the Spurs games Willie Henderson and Jimmy Millar scored in the 5-2 defeat at White Hart Lane and Ralph Brand and Davie Wilson scored at Ibrox in the 3-2 reverse.

HUGH BAIRD (Glasgow) Can you give the Wolves side against Rangers at Ibrox in the Cup Winners Cup of 1961? Did Billy Wright play for them? Was one of the Wolves players a well-known amateur?

Billy Wright was not in the Wolves side which read: Finlayson, Smart, Showell, Clamp, Slater, Flowers, Delley, Murray, Farmer, Mason, Durandt. The centre-half, Bill Slater played for some time at Wolverhampton as an amateur.

N. GRAY NEILSTON (Glasgow) When Rangers played Moscow Dynamo in the final of the European Cup Winners Cup in Barcelona was the match shown live or were recorded highlights shown?

This match, with Rangers winning 3-2, was played on May 24 1972 and recorded highlights were shown on BBC at 10.35p.m. with STV coming on five minutes earlier. On the same evening Scotland had beaten Wales 1-0 in an international match at Hampden Park.

CALLING DAVY M. (Kirkintilloch)
Teams in the first round of the European Cup Winners tie between Rangers and Dukla Prague at Ibrox on September 30, 1981 were, RANGERS, Stewart, McClelland, Dawson, Jardine, Forsyth, Bett, Cooper, Russell, McAdam, MacDonald, Johnston. DUKLA PRAGUE, Netolika, Macela, Kapko, Fiala, Rada, Kozak, Vizek, Rott, Nehoda, Kriz, Stambachr. Scorers for Rangers were Bett and MacDonald while Stambachr had the Czechs' only goal.

KNOW NOTHING (Drumchapel) Have Borussia Munchengladbach ever beaten Rangers 8-1 in a European Cup match? I say yes, my pal no.
You're aptly named I'm afraid. In season 1960-61 the clubs met in the Cup Winners trophy. Rangers won 11-0 on aggregate including an 8-0 success at Ibrox. Perhaps you have reversed the two scores in your mind.

JOCKY LAD (Dreghorn) Is it true that Willie Henderson's first goal in Europe was a perfectly good goal but nevertheless did not count?
I assume you have in mind that in season 1961-62 Rangers had to play both matches against Vorwaerts of East Germany in Europe because of political difficulties. After winning 2-1 in East Germany it was decided to play the "home leg" in Sweden. With Rangers leading 1-0 by a Henderson goal the game had to be abandoned because of dense fog. The game was played the following morning, Rangers winning very comfortably by 4-1.

JOHN and IAN (Elcho Bar) At which end did Puskas of Real Madrid score the only goal in the European Cup tie against Rangers in 1963? How long was there to go?
This goal was scored at the Copland Road end of the ground and was timed at 87 minutes.

MRS. M. G. ROBERTSON (Glasgow) Have Rangers ever played in a competitive European match in Northern Ireland? If so, please give details of the Rangers team, score and competition.

This was a European Cup Winners tie against Glentoran played at The Oval on September 27, 1966. The Rangers team in a 1-1 draw was, Ritchie, Johansen, Provan, Millar, McKinnon, D Smith, Henderson, Greig, McLean, A Smith, Johnston. George McLean scored for Rangers and Sinclair equalised for Glentoran.

CHAPTER SIX

Light Blues in Dark Blue

Over the last 120 years it has been true to say that a strong Rangers has meant a strong Scotland. Scores of Rangers players have worn the dark blue and in fact no fewer than 25 Rangers have had the supreme honour of captaining their country.

Some of the achievments have been truly remarkable, such as Alan Morton's 11 caps against England in the days when the English game was the one international that really counted. George Young has captained Scotland almost more times than the other 24 Rangers players put together. He was an astonishing skipper, by common consent there has never been anyone remotely like him for making nervous debutants at ease with their intimidating new surroundings. In deportment and field discipline he was a model for any youngster. I saw him play over fully 15 years and would swear in court that never ONCE in that time did I see him deliberately foul an opponent. He had a curious ability to raise his game in international matches. Often his club form would be comparatively indifferent and when the Scotland team was announced the thought surfaced, "Would he have made the team had he been playing for Morton or Aberdeen?" Yet on the day he would do what was necessary and another top-notch English or Continental forward would have been subdued. He was a less flamboyant captain than his immediate predecessor Jock Shaw but none the less effective for that.

Not everyone could make the jump from club to international

football. Among those who did not was Dougie Gray who season-in, season-out was unfailingly the best right back in club football but seemed nervous and tentative in a Scotland shirt. Perhaps he needed a longer run, over three or four consecutive games say, and in this the custom of not picking the strongest sides against Wales or Ireland did not do anything for continuity.

International sides in the years up to 1965 were selected by a Committee and there were almost always a couple of comparatively unknown Anglos who seemed to be picked for no better reason than to justify the jaunts of the selectors to England. Such as Ian Black of Southampton, Neil Dougall of Birmingham City and Willie Moir of Bolton Wanderers became known, slightly unfairly, as the "one-cap wonders".

While this was going on, the greatest Scottish centre-forward of all time, Jimmy McGrory, and the best Scottish inside-forward between the wars, Bob McPhail, did not record a single appearance at Wembley between them, although Bob McPhail might confess, under pressure, that at least one of his non-appearances was caused by Bill Struth telling him to save himself for a forthcoming Cup Final.

Great performances linger in the memory, notably Jim Baxter's two goals against England in 1963, after a fearful injury to Eric Caldow, the second serious injury to a Rangers player at Wembley as Sammy Cox had taken a bad knock in 1953. The calm composure of Baxter remains vivid as does his astonishing display of keepy-uppy in the match four years later which saw Scotland defeat the then World Cup champions England by 3-2. Not all his team-mates appreciated his cheek at the time. Denis Law will tell you that on that afternoon he could have seen Jim's tricks and cantrips far enough! Davie Wilson too deserves our eternal remembrance for the splendid way in which he assumed Eric Caldow's duties at full-back.

Not everybody coped so well with the peculiar pressures of Wembley and certainly Stewart Kennedy will not have happy memories of his one appearance there, a great shame for such a day should be the highlight of any player's career. There have been great international goals scored at Hampden by Rangers players. That secured by Eric Caldow in April 1962 was merely a conventional penalty but it meant that Scotland would beat the Auld Enemy at Hampden for the first time in 25 years. More flamboyant was the well-worked goal which John Greig scored against Italy with a couple of minutes to go and which kept our 1966 World Cup hopes alive for a few months more.

There was an Ibrox conveyor-belt of brilliant right wingers by which Waddell became Scott became Henderson, and this at a time when the opposition for that spot was quite awesome. With Jimmy Delaney, Gordon Smith, Graham Leggatt and Jimmy Johnstone all being in contention there was no doubt about it, whoever was Scotland's right-winger in the years between 1945-70 was entitled to feel he had won the position the hard way.

Rangers of course had for long provided Irish internationalists as well, and in recent years with the arrival of foreign players that representation has been extended to several European and Commonwealth countries. We sometimes read that footballers today are merely hardened and cynical mercenaries but I have never seen one who took his first cap for granted.

One of the most moving things I have ever heard was told to me by Bob McPhail. I asked him what had been the highlight of his football career. Bear in mind that this was a man who had scores of caps, half a dozen cup medals with Rangers and one with Airdrie and more League medals than he knew what to do with. In addition he had played against the English legends, men such as Harry Hibbs and Dixie Dean, Eddie Hapgood and Stan Matthews. And did he choose any of these? He did not. In reply to my question he said simply, "When I was picked to play for Scotland as a schoolboy against the Welsh Schools in Wales and travelled in a corridor train for the first time in my life to represent my country."

Four Rangers managers, Waddell, Symon, Souness and Greig have been internationalists, three of them on a very regular basis, Symon capped only once but certainly the intrusion of the Second World War had something to do with that. Today it becomes more difficult to balance the competing interests of club and country. Certainly there are too many internationals and against some very small and indifferent countries at that. The money is with the big clubs, but despite that, any Rangers player worth his keep will be just as keen to wear the national shirt in the future as any of those who went before him.

INTERNATIONAL CALLS

WELLPARK (Glasgow) Is it true that Alex Scott of Rangers was capped against England while playing in the reserves and is this a record?

Scott was picked against England in 1960 when Willie Henderson had played in three of the last four matches before the international side was selected. I can't think of another Scottish player off-hand in that position but of course Pat Bonner has been in a similar position as regards Celtic and the Republic of Ireland. It is certainly an unusual occurrence.

BIG HOPE BOBBY (Glasgow) Did Jim Baxter play in the Aberfan Disaster match against Wales and did he play in all three Home International matches in that season, 1966-67?

He was at inside-left against Wales at Cardiff in a 1-1 draw on October 22, 1966, the Aberfan Disaster weekend. He was then left out of the side which beat Ireland 2-1 at Hampden on November 16 but returned against England at left-half to play his part in the 3-2 defeat of world champions England at Wembley in April 1967.

TOM BOY (Linwood) How many Rangers players were in the Scotland side against Holland in 1968 and who was the international team manager at the time?

Former Ranger Bobby Brown was in command and he picked four Ibrox men, Greig, McKinnon, D Smith and Mathieson.

GOODHAND TAIT (Cathcart) Who was the Scotland scorer when they lost 4-1 to England at Wembley in 1969 and what was unusual about the fixture?

Colin Stein of Rangers was our scorer, heading an Eddie Gray cross past England goalkeeper Gordon Banks. The game was played on a Saturday but it had an evening kick-off.

RIVETER (Springburn) I am looking for an international match which seems to have "got lost". It was the Burnden Park Disaster match of 1946 and could you give me the score, the Scotland team and the number of Rangers players involved.

This match was played at Manchester at the start of the 1946-47 season and was a 2-2 draw. The Scotland side was, Miller (Celtic), D Shaw (Hibernian), J Shaw (Rangers), Campbell (Morton), Brennan (Newcastle United), Husband (Partick Thistle), Waddell (Rangers), Dougal (Birmingham), Thornton (Rangers), Hamilton (Aberdeen), Liddell (Liverpool).

Scorer for Scotland was Thornton (2), and for England Welsh (2, 1 pen). You will see that there were three Rangers players in the side.

McGOWAN (Ruchazie) Did Jerry Dawson keep goal against England at Hampden in 1937 and did he ever play at Wembley in a full international? Did Sandy Archibald ever play at Wembley in a full international?

Jerry Dawson played in the 3-1 victory over England at Hampden in 1937. He was also in the side which got a 1-1 draw at Wembley the year before. Sandy Archibald was at outside-right in the very first meeting of the countries at Wembley in 1924, a match which was also a 1-1 draw.

GWAN YA BEAUTY (Troon) I say that when Scotland beat England 3-1 at Wembley in 1949 Willie Woodburn was at centre-half in an all Old Firm half-back line.

Willie was certainly at centre-half but his wing-halves that day were Bobby Evans of Celtic and George Aitken of East Fife.

BROADCROFTER (Queenzieburn) How many Rangers players were in the Scotland side which beat Czechoslovakia in 1973 when Joe Jordan came on as substitute?

Sandy Jardine at right-back was the lone Ranger on that particular night.

WEE TAM (Dunlop) Did Jerry Dawson keep goal for

Scotland in the last four international matches against England before the Second World War?

No. He was in goal in 1936, 1937 and 1939 but in 1938 he had been badly injured and his place in goal was taken by Dave Cumming of Middlesbrough who had formerly kept goal with Aberdeen and Arbroath.

CHAPTER SEVEN

Attendances

Now You Know readers are fascinated by attendances, not in the least surprising when you reckon that for the first fifty years of this century Glasgow was the football capital of Britain and therefore by extension of the world. Around the turn of the century the city had four grounds which could hold upwards of 40,000 people, a provision that no other city in Europe could look at.

As what has normally been the most strongly-supported club in the land it is not astonishing that Rangers have helped to establish most of the crowd records that there are – with the exception of the biggest single crowd for a Scottish Cup Final. In these days of drastically reduced attendances that particular record can never be achieved.

There are plenty of others around. There is the record for a Scottish Cup final and replay in aggregate. There is the record for a Scottish Cup tie apart from a final match. There is the record for a floodlit friendly match and there is the all-time Scottish League record, the Old Firm fixture of January 1939 providing the only instance of a six-figure crowd at a Scottish League match.

More interesting to modern readers is the week-in week-out attendance of 40,000 plus at home matches, assisted greatly by the unprecedented number of season-ticket holders. Of course such phenomenal ticket sales are only made possible by success on the park. When the club was in the doldrums in the early 1980s the core support at home matches bottomed out on the 15,000 mark.

Fans also want to know about low attendances and these are much more difficult to quantify. End of season matches in a bad season have been put at around 3,000 but this is almost certainly too low and has tended to be based on estimates rather than on official figures. There have been one or two oddities where Rangers have played to very small gates but there has almost always been a specific reason for this. Thus a European Cup tie against Vorwaerts of East Germany attracted a crowd put at between 2,500 and 3,500 but because of political considerations the match had to be played on neutral ground in Sweden. Again, a crowd of 11,000 at a home tie in a European competition may not seem very much but it becomes remarkable when one realises that it was a second-leg tie and Rangers were already eight goals up on their Maltese opposition when it started.

Fashions change in football, and now that we have European competition the occasional friendly matches are less attractive. The limitations on ground size in the wake of the effect of the Taylor Report on British football (its recommendations are not obligatory on Scottish football but will obviously be very influential) mean that increasingly small is beautiful.

Nor should we confine ourselves purely to first-team matches.

As recently as this year it was demonstrated that around 20,000 people would turn up at Ibrox to see an Old Firm reserve match and until the 1960s even the pre-season trial would attract anything between 10,000 and 15,000 spectators. When we look back at the Ibrox of the 1940s it appears very spartan to us in comparison with today's magnificent ground but both designs have one thing in common – more often than not the sold-out notices went up and go up.

WEE WULLIE (Barrhead) Is it true that during the Second World War there was a Rangers-Celtic game at Hampden with an all-ticket limit of less than 20,000?

When Rangers met Celtic in the semi-final of the Glasgow Cup at Hampden on Monday 29 September 1941 there was an all-ticket limit of 15,000. This had been ordered by the then Chief Constable Percy Sillitoe as a result of crowd trouble at a previous game.

RANGERS DAFT (Stonehouse) What was the record attendance at Ibrox and who provided the opposition?

The match was on January 2, 1939 when Rangers beat Celtic 2-1 before a record attendance of 118,567.

ANGUS BAR (Coatbridge) I maintain that Rangers hold the record gate for any club match in Britain. I think the game was against Hibs.

This is not quite correct. The two teams you mention hold the record for any club match in Britain apart from the final of a national competition. The Scottish Cup semi-final of 1948 between Hibernian and Rangers drew a massive 143,570 to Hampden.

BIG J and WEE J (Glasgow) Did Rangers ever play before a crowd of 500 in a European Cup tie?

No. You have in mind I think the second-leg second-round tie against Vorwaerts of East Germany in the European Cup of 1961-62. This match had to be played at Malmo in Sweden as Vorwaerts had been refused permission to come to Britain. The attendance was therefore very small but even at that was quoted at 1,800.

THE GEORGE (Port Glasgow) What was the aggregate attendance for the Scottish Cup final of 1948, what were the scores and did both matches go to extra time?

The aggregate attendances at this final between Rangers and Morton was 265,199. The first game was a 1-1 draw after extra time and the replay was a 1-0 win for Rangers, also in extra time. Billy Williamson got the winner in his only Cup appearance that season.

**BROWNBANK (Paisley) Apart from the famous Old Firm
match of 1939 have Rangers ever played to another six figure
crowd at Ibrox?**

*They have on at least one occasion. The gate in the Scottish
Cup tie against Hibernian in 1951 was given as being in excess
of 102,000. There may well be other instances but this should
settle your bet for you.*

CHAPTER EIGHT

High Scores, High Scorers

Any supporter worth his salt is going to be interested in high scores and emphatic wins by his side. That is not to say that these represent the best performances by his favourites, certainly they do not in the case of Rangers. Such scores as 13-0 against both Possilpark and Uddingston in the Scottish Cup of 1878, of 11-0 against Whitehill in 1885, of 11-1 against Edinburgh City and 14-2 against Blairgowrie in the Scottish Cups of 1929 and 1934 respectively tell us more of the calibre of the opposition than of the home side's ability. To beat the great Motherwell side of the time 5-2 at Fir Park in the Scottish Cup of 1930 was comparatively an infinitely superior performance while the 6-1 win against Aberdeen in the semi-final of the Scottish Cup at Parkhead in 1969 was even more remarkable.

League victories are a more reliable guide since by definition both teams are operating on the same grade. Therefore the wins over Airdrie by 8-2 in season 1952-53, the 8-0 defeat of Queen of the South in 1955-56 and the 10-2 thrashing of Raith Rovers in season 1967-68 must rank very high on the list of scoring achievements.

Some of the early tours of Canada provided opportunities for high-scoring but Jerry Dawson compared these matches to shooting fish in a barrel and obviously did not rank the skills of the opposition sides very highly This impression might be strengthened by the fact that on this tour in 1930 Rangers scored

68 goals in 14 matches, but in fairness it has to be said that the touring side faced difficulties. If they ran up a cricket score then the opposition was no good. Equally if they took their foot off the pedal they were accused of not trying and of condescension to their hosts.

The broadening of the frontiers which European competition brought in every sense led to some highly competent performances. Among these were the 8-0 pounding of Borussia in the European Cup Winners Cup at Ibrox in 1960-61, the 4-0 defeat of Seville in the same competition in 1963 and the 5-2 defeat of the powerful Belgian side Anderlecht in the major competition, the European Cup in 1959-60 and then 2-0 away. Such results were worth ten of the overwhelming victory secured against a hopelessly mismatched Maltese team some 25 years later.

Fondest of all large-scale victories of course is the 8-1 success against Celtic on January 1, 1943 even although this was not an official Scottish League match. In recent years, as teams have learned to play defensively – and it is always easier to coach defence – the number of really big scores has tended to decrease so that nowadays 4-0 would be regarded as very handsome and 6-0 as quite exceptional.

The great goal scorers speak for themselves of course, McPhail, Thornton, Derek Johnstone, McCoist, Hateley, although curiously it was sometimes other players who stole the headlines with outstanding one-off performances. Thus Davie Wilson had six goals in a First Division League match at Falkirk. Derek Parlane had four in an away match at Dunfermline and as has been mentioned elsewhere, Don Kichenbrand scored five in the first-ever floodlit league match in Scotland. In Europe, and making allowances for the lowly class of the opposition, Dave McPherson somewhat improbably had four goals in the away match against Valetta in Malta. With the recent break-up of many European countries into their constituent parts it may be that we shall see further startling feats of scoring in Europe so that even Rangers away record of eight goals in Malta may be overtaken by the club.

For those who already think football is a funny game, here is an oddity. When the Scottish League Cup started in 1946-47 it was three years before Rangers lost three goals at Ibrox and then it was to Cowdenbeath of all teams. Five years went by before Clyde equalled this total and then after the years of shut-outs and near shut-outs, Falkirk scored three the following year and Celtic four. In 1964 Rangers would make the headlines by recording a 9-1 away victory in the League Cup over St Johnstone at Perth, comfortably their best result in this competition.

BUCHANAN COOPERAGE (Stepps) I say Willie Miller was not in goal for Celtic when Rangers beat them 8-1. Please give both teams.

> *He was. Teams in this Southern League match of January 1, 1943 were, RANGERS, Dawson, Gray, Shaw, Little, Young, Symon, Waddell, Duncanson, Gillick, Venters, Johnstone.*
> *CELTIC, Miller, McDonald, Dornan, Lynch, Corbett, Paterson, Delaney, McAuley, Airlie, McGowan, Duncan.*

Calling CHARLES SHARPE (Glasgow)

> *Thank you for your letter in which you point out that Jimmy Fleming had six goals against Clyde in a Glasgow Cup match in season 1927-28 and that Don Kichenbrand had five against Queen of the South in a midweek league match at Ibrox .*

PARTICK GARAGE (Glasgow) How many goals did Colin Stein score in his first three games for Rangers? When did he make his last appearance for them?

> *In his first match against Arbroath at Gayfield on November 2, 1968 he had three goals in a 5-1 win. He also had three in the next league match against Hibernian who lost at Ibrox 6-1 and he scored two in a mid-week match against Dundalk in a European tie. In his third league game (I am not sure if you are thinking only of league games) Rangers lost 1-0 to St Mirren at Paisley. His last game was in a 3-1 defeat in the league by Celtic at Hampden (note the venue) on September 16, 1972.*

D. D. L. (Govan) Please give the number of goals scored for Rangers by Bob McPhail.

*In a career at Ibrox which stretched from 1927 to 1940 Bob
McPhail in 466 matches recorded the extremely high tally of
281 goals.*

**EDMISTON EDDIE (Kinning Park) Who were the leading
scorers for Rangers in season 1929-30?**

*Jimmy Fleming was way out in front with 33, Bob McPhail had
19, Alan Morton 14 and Sandy Archibald 12.*

**SWINGER (Kincardine) Have Rangers ever scored five goals
in a league match and failed to win it? If so oblige with details.**

*There was a 5-5 draw with Falkirk at Brockville on March 14,
1959 and these were the teams, FALKIRK, Slater, Richmond,
Rae, Price, Prentice, McMillan, Murray, Wright, White, Moran,
Oliver.*

*RANGERS, Niven, Shearer, Caldow, Davis, Telfer, Stevenson,
Scott, McMillan, Murray, Brand, Wilson.*

**JOHN MARKIE (Cove Bay) Please give dates teams and scorers
in a match between Rangers and Raith Rovers at Ibrox which
Rangers won 10-3. I say that Ian Porterfield who later managed
Aberdeen scored one of the Raith Rovers goals that day.**

*The match was played in December 1967 with Rangers winning
10-2 (note the score) and Ian Porterfield did not score. Teams
were, RANGERS, Sorensen, Johansen, Mathieson, Greig,
McKinnon, D Smith, Penman, Willoughby, Ferguson, Johnston,
Persson.*

*RAITH ROVERS, J Gray, Hislop, A Gray, Stein, Davidson,
Porterfield, Lister, Sneddon, Wallace, Cunningham, Falconer.
For Rangers Ferguson (3), Persson (2), Greig (2), Johnston (2),
and Willoughby all found the net with the Raith goals coming
from Lister and D Smith, o.g.*

**T. B. (Knightswood) Can you confirm that Willie Johnston
scored nine times at Parkhead in the course of a single season?**

*Not quite. He had two goals against Celtic in a 4-2 League win,
three against them in a 4-3 Glasgow Cup success and three
against Aberdeen in a 6-1 Scottish Cup semi-final tie for which
Parkhead was the venue. All this took place in season 1968-69.*

KNOXY and DANCER (Yarrows) My mate says Alex Scott got

four goals playing at centre-forward in a match against Ayr United. I say he got three.

You win. Scott had three goals in a 7-3 defeat of Ayr United at Ibrox on April 29, 1961 Wilson and Brand each recording a brace.

DAVID STEVENSON (Muirhead) In a league match, around 1971 did Willie Johnston come on as a substitute and score a hat-trick of penalties against St Johnstone?

To my considerable surprise the answer is yes. On November 6, 1971 he came on as substitute for Graham Fyfe and scored three from the spot in a 4-1 win, all the goals coming in the second-half.

STATUS QUO (Port Glasgow) Did Rangers ever face Edinburgh City in a competitive match? I say they did not.

They did. In a first-round Scottish Cup tie at Ibrox in 1929 Rangers thrashed the amateurs from the East of Scotland 11-1.

Calling SELDOM BULLY WEE (Oatlands)

I have traced the high-scoring Glasgow Cup tie between Clyde and Rangers immediately following the Second World War. It was played at Shawfield on September 23, 1945 and Clyde won 4-3. Their scorers were Riley, Dixon (2), and Campbell with Williamson, Venters and Gillick counting for Rangers. Hickie missed a penalty for Clyde who were beaten 2-0 in the final by Queen's Park.

WEE MOORE (Cambuslang) How many goals did Colin Stein score in his time with Rangers and how did this compare with his performance as a Hibernian player?

In 111 matches plus one substitution he scored 59 goals for Rangers compared with 40 goals in 69 games while he was a Hibernian player.

CHAPTER NINE

Floodlights

It comes as something of a shock to Now You Know readers to
learn that the answer to the question, "When was the first football
match played under artificial lighting in Scotland?" is "More than
a century ago." In the last years of the nineteenth century several
matches were played under arc lights or Wells lights as they were
known and the results would have been perfectly satisfactory
except for the proliferation of overhead cables.

Possibly it was the severity of the climate which discouraged
the experiment as it might have been thought that it would deter
spectators from going out to stand on winter nights in grounds
which were largely uncovered. It was the success of baseball
matches under floodlights in the USA in the 1930s which rekindled
the notion that this might work for football although of course the
Second World War and the consequent black-out held matters
up here for another 15 years or so.

So when did Rangers get involved with floodlit football? Well,
it depends what you mean. There had been experimental matches
with mixed Rangers sides as early as 1953. Ibrox presented
technical difficulties because of its nearness to Glasgow Airport,
which in those days was a couple of miles nearer the city at
Renfrew. River mist and fog had also to be taken into consideration
and Rangers were almost alone among major Scottish and English
clubs in not going for the conventional pylon system.

The first big floodlight match was a friendly against English rivals of long standing, Arsenal doing the opening honours. And in 1955-56 the first league match under floodlights in Scotland featured Rangers and Queen of the South at Ibrox. The home side took to the new medium right away and none more so than Don Kichenbrand who had a nap hand of goals and attracted such forgettable headlines as, "The rhino comes out at night."

It was clear that there was an enormous public for such matches and an added impetus was given by the development of European competitions just at this time and over the 40 years or so since, there have been many memorable nights under the lights, notably the 2-0 win against Wolves and the narrow 1-0 loss to Real Madrid. Even those were put in the shade in season 1992-93 when no one fortunate enough to be there will forget the gritty recovery against Marseilles and the Scott Nisbet goal which brought victory against Bruges.

A great floodlit honour came Rangers way when in 1961 they were invited to open the Hampden floodlights which had been surprisingly long in arriving, with a match against their great European opponents, Eintracht Frankfurt. For the only time in recorded football history a friendly floodlit match attracted a six-figure crowd although with Eintracht three up at one stage visions of another rout flitted before everyone's eyes. Rangers battled on and two goals from a very improbable source, Harry Davis, meant that honour was saved even if the match was not quite salvaged.

For almost half a century the roads out of the city centre have been jam-packed on big match nights, too much so for poor Willie Henderson who suffered the tortures of the damned when in 1962 the breakdown of a friend's car caused him to arrive at Ibrox too late to play in the return leg of the tie with Standard Liege which began with Rangers 4-1 down. On their own patch Rangers won 2-0 so the absence of Henderson may well have been crucial.

The introduction of floodlighting transformed the game. Strips were altered to take account of it and the later kick-offs in winter allowed fans to travel from further afield when people still worked on Saturday mornings. Above all, it allowed the Scots football follower to see at regular intervals the cream of European footballers and to judge how the domestic game stood in relation to them.

JASPER (Glenboig) Please oblige with the Rangers and Arsenal teams at the first floodlit game at Ibrox. Was there a record turn out?

On December 8, 1953 Arsenal beat Rangers 2-1 before a record crowd of 70,000 for a floodlit game in Britain. Teams were, RANGERS, Brown, Young, Little, McColl, Stanners, Cox, Waddell, Grierson, Simpson, Thornton, McCulloch.

ARSENAL, Kelsey, Wills, Smith, Forbes, Dodgin, Mercer, Milton, Logie, Halton, Lawton, Roper.

NED (Ibrox) Can you name the first Scottish club to use floodlighting. I say Dumbarton, my friend says Airdrieonians.

Floodlighting was first used for two schools' matches at Broomfield. The first floodlit match involving senior clubs was played at Ochilview on November 19, 1952 when Rangers beat Stenhousemuir 2-0.

GLENKIRK (Troon) What teams played in the very first experimental floodlit game at Ibrox?

This match took place on November 25, 1952 when Rangers fielded two sides in a match entitled Whites v Stripes.

Chapter ten

The Great Veterans

There was a time when long service and Rangers went hand in hand, very wisely too for one of the most important things in supporting a club is that players and supporters should be able to put down roots in their acquaintanceship. It was of course exceptional for players like Alec Smith before 1914 and Dougie Gray between the wars to clock up more than 20 years, an astonishing length in a career as short as that of a professional footballer. But from 1920 to 1960, Rangers players with 15 years or more were commonplace. Dawson, Shaw, Young, Woodburn, Waddell, Thornton, Ian McColl would all fall into this category as, a little earlier would have done Davie Meiklejohn, Bob McPhail and Sandy Archibald.

When I took over the column it was remarkable how many people still wrote of Dougie Gray who perhaps alone among all these star names had an undistinguished international career (he might well have been given more opportunities) but yet was the model of the dependable club man. He was never out of the Rangers side unless injured and his haul of six Scottish Cup medals and eleven championships speaks for itself. Bob McPhail added

Opposite
Ian McMillan, secure in Ibrox legend as the Wee Prime Minister and an excellent example of the classic ball-playing Scottish inside-forward

six cup medals to the one he already had at Broomfield and his 14 years service is quite remarkable in that he was already very much an established player with Airdrie before joining Rangers.

John Greig's 18 years is quite phenomenal given that he was playing in the faster much more competitive modern game and encountering European competition at club and national level, something which his distinguished predecessors had never been called upon to do. Such a record would have been impossible without an extraordinary enthusiasm for the game and a willingness to meet the rigorous physical standards imposed.

Extrovert players such as John Greig are impossible to ignore, others, quieter, establish long-service records almost by stealth and one example of this would be Peter McCloy who had the strength of character to fight his way back to first team duty after apparently having lost his place permanently.

The long servers are few in number these days because the game has changed. At top level, any player capable of it sees a spell in Europe as high on his list of priorities. More than any other clubs the Old Firm can retain the loyalty of their players but even at that it would be foolish not to recognise that the game is more mercenary than it was. Again, the demands of Europe make it imperative that there should be at least some Continental ingredient to the make-up of the side and in the nature of things Europeans seldom spend more than five years or so in British football.

A long-serving player now tends to be someone who gets into double figures with his club in years of service and of the present squad at Ibrox only Ally McCoist and Ian Durrant come into this category. The long-serving player has a great role to play. Fathers can introduce him to sons and they supply that continuity which is an important part of the game. It is hard to form any rapport with players who, as in the case of some clubs, seem to arrive and leave by means of a revolving door.

J. D. (Bridgeton) When was Willie Woodburn's suspension lifted?

In November 1955 the SFA Referee Committee decided that Willie Woodburn could take part in football in any capacity other than as a player. In April 1957 the suspension was completely lifted but Woodburn decided not to play again.

BARCELONA TOMMY (Glasgow) How many appearances did the following players make for Rangers, Davie Meiklejohn, Sandy Archibald and George Young?

Meiklejohn had 635 competitive matches with Rangers, Archibald made 667 appearances and George Young edged him out with 678.

CROW BAR (Kilmarnock) When did Jim Baxter play his last league game for Rangers? Did he play after the Ibrox Disaster?

I make his last league game to have been against Aberdeen at Ibrox on December 20, 1969. Baxter was at inside-right to Willie Henderson and Rangers won 3-2. He did not play after the Ibrox Disaster in January 1971.

BLACK LABEL (Glasgow) Details please of Jimmy Millar's last game for Rangers.

Jimmy's last game in a first team jersey was at Perth on November 12, 1966 in a 1-1 draw with St Johnstone in a league match.

G. O'N. (Glasgow) Date, opposition, venue and scorers for Alec Scott's debut for Rangers.

This was a midweek league game at Ibrox against Falkirk on March 10, 1955. Rangers won 4-1, their scorers being Gardiner and Scott (3), with Alec McCrae scoring for the Bairns.

W. N. R. (Glasgow) Of Jim Forrest's 56 goals in season 1964-65 how many were in European matches? What was Sam English's best goal scoring season in league football?

Jim Forrest scored six European goals in 1964-65. Sam English still holds the record number of league goals with 44 in season 1931-32.

BET (Coatbridge) When did Alan Morton begin and end with Rangers?

Curiously the venue and the opposition were the same on both occasions, against Airdrie at Ibrox on August 17, 1920 and on January 7, 1933.

HENRY KETTLE (Drumoyne) Who is the longest-ever serving Rangers player, is it Alec Smith or Dougie Gray?

Alec Smith signed on April 30, 1894 and was a Ranger until 1915. Dougie Gray signed from Aberdeen Mugiemoss in 1925 and was freed at the end of April 1947. Gray appears to have been there for almost a year longer than Smith.

THE SEAL (Dreghorn) Did Willie Woodburn ever play at centre-forward for Rangers in a first-team match?

He played at least once in that position in the war-time Southern League. This was a match against Motherwell at Ibrox in September 1944 and he was in direct opposition to Andy Paton.

WEE MAN (Holytown) How long was Willie Henderson with Rangers?

He signed from Edinburgh Athletic in August 1960 and joined Sheffield Wednesday in July 1972.

DON REX (Erskine) When did Jimmy Duncanson sign for Rangers and did he play with any other Scottish clubs?

Signed from Dunoon Milton Rovers in 1938 Duncanson had a season with Hamilton Academicals during the war and at the end of his career had a brief spell with St Mirren. I have a notion he may have turned out in a couple of games with Stranraer just before hanging up the boots.

PETER WHITE (Grangemouth) When Willie Henderson took over at outside-right for Rangers how long was it until Alec Scott was transferred to Everton?

Signed for Rangers in 1960 Henderson had pretty well

*established himself as first choice by the end of season 1961-62.
Alec Scott signed for Everton in February 1963.*

**JOHNNY ONE-EYE (Saltcoats) Did Davie Meiklejohn ever
play in opposition to Alan Morton in senior football?**

*No. The only time they might have been opponents was in season
1919-20 and Meiklejohn did not play in either of the Queen's
Park matches that year.*

Calling WELLPARK (Glasgow)

*You are wrong in thinking that Jock Shaw had left Ibrox towards
the end of the 1940s. He remained a Rangers player until season
1953-54 as I said.*

**NELG (Govan) When did Bob McPhail join Rangers and was
he ever a team-mate of George McQueen at Ibrox?**

*Bob McPhail joined Rangers in April 1927 some time after
George McQueen had left Ibrox.*

**JOCKY (Glasgow) When did Bobby Brown play his last first-
team game for Rangers?**

*He did not leave Ibrox until the end of season 1956-57 but his
last first-team game was well before that on January 21, 1956
when he was in the Rangers side which beat East Fife 3-0 in a
league match at Ibrox.*

**J. McG. (Patterton) How long was Tommy Muirhead at Ibrox,
how many goals did he score and what was his subsequent
career?**

*He arrived at Ibrox in 1917-18 and was then in the forces until
1919. He was thereafter a regular Rangers player until season
1929-30. In all he scored 49 goals. Later he managed St
Johnstone in the 1930s and for many years after that was a
well-known sports journalist.*

**C. F. CAMPBELL (Liverpool) Was Alan Morton still a Queen's
Park player in August 1919? How long was he at Hampden
altogether?**

*Alan Morton did not move to Ibrox until the summer of 1920
by which time he had been almost seven years at Hampden. As
he was a Rangers player until 1933 this meant that he spent
more than 20 years in top class football.*

A. G. (Ayr) When did Jim Baxter make his first competitive appearance for Rangers and what position did he fill?

He made his competitive debut in a League Cup tie against Partick Thistle at Ibrox on August 13 1961 and was at inside-left in a match which Rangers won 3-1.

CHAPTER ELEVEN

Quite Apart from the Football – Other Uses

Over the years Ibrox Stadium has hosted many other activities besides Association football. There were of course the Rangers sports which deserve a section to themselves but in addition title fights have been held at Ibrox as have professional tennis exhibitions.

Nor have all the other uses necessarily been sporting. Winston Churchill addressed a rally of Scottish Conservatives and Unionists in 1949. He was out of office at the time and Leader of the Opposition or he would have made the third prime minister to have visited Ibrox, the other two being Harold MacMillan and Margaret Thatcher. Two reigning monarchs have also been to the ground. In 1917 King George V conducted an investiture there at which many Scottish servicemen were decorated and in 1938 the stadium was chosen as the site for the opening of the Empire Exhibition by King George VI.

There have been religious revival rallies led by Dr Billy Graham, there have been parades of youth organisations such as the Boy Scouts and Boys Brigade. There was too in 1938 a series of military tattoos held as part of the Empire Exhibition. No doubt this seemed a good idea at the time but the light tanks which traversed the Ibrox turf for several nights in succession did nothing for the state of the pitch and perhaps fortunately the thoughts of the then groundsman remain unrecorded.

A non-football question that occasionally surfaces even yet is whether the great tennis player Fred Perry ever played at Ibrox in a tennis match. The answer is that he did not but efforts were made to get him to participate in a tennis tournament during the Empire Exhibition of 1938. In the event he did not come, nor did Henri Cochet the great French player who would certainly have been a draw. A tournament was however held from July 5 to July 7 with a wooden court being constructed in front of the main stand and a series of exhibition matches played . The leading light was the American Bill Tilden who had won the men's title at Wimbledon and there was also a very useful German player, Hans Nusslein.

It makes no sense at all to have a well-equipped stadium which is used only for a couple of hours every two weeks and in recent years Ibrox has hosted world title fights in which the great Scottish lightweight, Jim Watt was involved. Away from sport there have been rock concerts and the visit to Glasgow of such established favourites as Frank Sinatra. No doubt there are fresh uses in store for Ibrox and at the time of writing tentative enquiries had been made as to the possibility of locating an American football team there.

THE EMPIRE EXHIBITION OF 1938

TORRY PARTY (Drumoyne) Did Torry Gillick take part in the final of the Empire Exhibition tournament at Ibrox in 1938? Were any other ex-Rangers players involved in the tournament final?

Torry Gillick played in the first round for Everton against Rangers and in the semi-final against Aberdeen but he missed the final tie against Celtic. A team-mate of Gillick's in the Goodison Park side was inside-forward Alex Stevenson who had been at Ibrox about four years previously.

H. L. I. (Maryhill) Is it true that during the First World War the King visited Ibrox to give out medals?

On September 18, 1917 His Majesty King George V visited Ibrox Park and presented medals and decorations to servicemen and civilians.

PLASTER (Southside) Can you name any Rangers player who took part both in the Empire Exhibition tournament of 1938 and the Coronation Cup of 1953? Did anyone manage this?

Two players qualify but neither of them were Rangers players. Joe Mercer was with Everton in 1938 and Arsenal in 1953 while even more remarkably George Hamilton represented Aberdeen in both competitions.

CHAPTER TWELVE

The Strips

The classical Rangers strip was the light blue worn between the wars and for some time afterwards. The white shorts and above all the red-topped black stockings made for a pleasing and uncluttered outfit as a fashion editor might have said had she been given the job of designing strips. It was the alternative strips that evoked comment.

Rangers change strip was rather similar to Queen's Park's normal strip with narrow hoops on a white background except that in Rangers case the hoops were of light blue rather than black. This was the jersey worn when playing such sides as Queen of the South and St Johnstone in away league matches but it was never popular with supporters. They indeed often attributed powers of misfortune to it although there is no statistical evidence to show that the side did any worse when so attired.

Interestingly, Celtic supporters also attributed evil powers to their change strip. The "butchers strip" as it was called from its likeness to the butchers aprons of those days, finally won acceptance when it was worn in the creditable drawn match against the great Moscow Dynamo. Ironically this was just at the time when it lost favour with the club itself.

In the 1950s the Rangers alternative strip was for a time dark blue with broad red and white bands but although more flamboyant than the butcher's strip this never really caught on. In the 1960s some few matches were played in an all-white strip but this may have had more to do with the introduction of floodlights than anything else.

Now jerseys undergo slight changes at least every other year as they become more cluttered almost to the extent of being walking sandwich-boards with not a square inch left uncovered by stripe or chevron. Roll neck succeeds V neck and some clubs have actually re-introduced the old string collar. But there is still the scope for a jersey which is good to look at and the recent away strip of orange and blue stripes would provide an example of that.

Nevertheless, the bulk of Rangers supporters would probably still plump for the inter-war strip although in one famous match in the 1940s a mix-up over jerseys in a League Cup tie with Cowdenbeath led to the hasty acquisition of a set of jerseys from a neighbouring minor club and the provision of a jersey which had certainly not been designed for George Young's titanic frame.

CHAPTER THIRTEEN

Rangers and the League

Are Rangers the most successful league side in Scottish football? Have Rangers ever gone through a complete League season without dropping a point? Have Rangers ever shared a championship? Have Rangers ever won a title on goal difference? Have Rangers ever lost the flag on a deciding match? Within the last 30 years did Rangers only win 3 out of 20 league titles? Have Rangers ever won nine league titles in a row?

Let me put readers out of suspense by telling them that the answer to all these questions except the last is yes and the answer to the last one is yes and no. Before the First World War Rangers championships tended to come in clusters with four consecutive titles being followed by three back to back wins. It was between 1918 and 1939 that Rangers completely dominated league football in Scotland winning 15 championships as against five for Celtic and a solitary Motherwell success.

For the first seven years after the Second World War Hibernian were the great rivals although on one occasion an astonishing fit of nerves cost Dundee the title when Rangers could do very little to prevent it going to Dens Park. In the late 50s and early 60s Hearts emerged as the creditable challengers and the provincial sides such as Dundee and Kilmarnock recorded the occasional praiseworthy success but Rangers won at least in alternate years. Even during the Celtic nine in a row spell there was twice only two points between the sides and on one of those occasions in 1968 a 90th minute goal made it possible for Celtic to retain their title.

As the Celtic challenge weakened so Rangers had the satisfaction of taking the last First Division title in 1975 and the first Premier Division one but immediately new threats appeared above the horizon in Aberdeen and Dundee United, the so-called New Firm. This time another eight years would elapse before the league title came back to Ibrox and then Rangers began to make up for lost time. Graeme Souness won it in his first year. It went back to Parkhead and then Rangers embarked on a six in a row run which would exceed anything the club had ever done before and arguably would be the most meritorious performance ever in that it had been achieved against what were recognisably the 10 or 12 strongest clubs in Scotland.

Often it was not the other member of the Old Firm that pressed them hardest over the years, Airdrieonians, Motherwell and Kilmarnock were often cast in the unwilling role of bridesmaids although the two latter clubs at least knew the consolation of a solitary success. As far as consistency is concerned on only 13 occasions out of 97 have Rangers failed to finish in the first three places. Oddly enough four of those occasions were in successive seasons from 1982-83 to 1985-86 and they have only once finished as low as sixth. Should Rangers go on to top Celtic's nine in a row it is a fair bet that the postbag that week will be of record proportions.

THE LEAGUE

TORRANCE HOUSE (Glasgow) Give details of a match when Third Lanark drew 2-2 with Rangers at Cathkin Park but Rangers won the league. Did Jocky Henderson miss a penalty kick for Third Lanark and was one of their players injured?

The following sides drew 2-2 at Cathkin on May 1, 1950. THIRD LANARK, Goram, Balunas, Harrower, Orr, Christie, Mooney, Henderson, Mason, Cuthbertson, Dick, Staroscik. RANGERS, Brown, Young, Shaw, McColl, Woodburn, Cox, Rutherford, Paton, Thornton, Williamson, Johnson. Scorers were Mason and Cuthbertson for Third Lanark and Williamson and Christie, o. g. for Rangers. Henderson did miss a penalty for Third Lanark and Mooney suffered a broken arm. The Third Lanark goalkeeper in this match was the father of the present Rangers keeper, Andy Goram.

P. D. (Garnethill) I know that early in their history Rangers won a league championship without dropping a single point. Who were in the league at that time and how many matches were played?

There were ten clubs in the League at that time so therefore 18 matches were played. The other nine sides were Hearts, Celtic, Hibernian, St Mirren, Third Lanark, Clyde, St Bernard, Partick Thistle and Dundee.

TASSIE GAMBLER (Glasgow) Please tell me the teams and goal scorers in the 1968 league match at Parkhead when Rangers won 4-2.

This match was played in September 1968 and the teams were, CELTIC, Simpson, Gemmell, O'Neill, Brogan, McNeill, Clark, Johnstone, Lennox, Wallace, Connolly, Hughes. RANGERS, Martin, Jackson, Mathieson, Greig, McKinnon, Hynd, Henderson, Penman, Jardine, Johnstone, Persson. Scorer for Celtic was Wallace (2), while for Rangers Johnstone (2), Persson and Penman found the net.

DIAMOND DONALD (Plains) I say that Airdrie once scored

four second-half goals in a match against Rangers at Ibrox. Can you confirm this?

It happened on October 8, 1955. In a truly remarkable 4-4 draw, all eight goals were scored in the last 39 minutes. Murray, Hubbard (2, 1 pen.) and Baird scored for Rangers with McCulloch (2), Reid and Rankin on the mark for Airdrie. The match was a league fixture.

K. P. (Kirkintilloch) What was the side that Davy Wilson of Rangers scored six goals against while playing at centre-forward? Was the match a mid-week game?

In season 1961-62 on Saturday March 17 Davy Wilson had six goals in a 7-1 win over Falkirk at Brockville.

CHAPTER FOURTEEN

European Players – the Continental Invasion

From the letters of many correspondents, it is obvious that they think that the influx of players from Europe is something which has started only in the last few years. Not so. For the better part of 30 years now a steady supply of players has arrived from the north of the continent.

Indeed, the forerunner goes back much further than that, to 1922 in fact, when the gifted Carl Hansen arrived from Copenhagen. He was to know a fair measure of success and scored in an Old Firm match when Rangers did the league double in season 1922-23 but a bad leg break in an alliance game in 1924 meant the end of his Ibrox career.

The next arrival came from even further north. Albert Gudmundsson was a slow but clever Icelander brought to Glasgow by war work in 1943. His studious kind of play was much appreciated although his appearances were entirely confined to the second team who were then playing in the North-Eastern league. Astonishingly, this small island was to provide another player in the mid 1960s when Thorolf Beck made the short trip from Paisley and St Mirren.

By that time Scotland was undergoing a considerable immigration from Scandinavia where as the game was still amateur, the leading players were increasingly going abroad.

Morton and Dundee United were the leading importers, closely followed by Hearts. Rangers took the two Sorensens who had both gained experience with Morton. Eric was a dashing continental style goalkeeper of great courage, Jorn Sorensen was a clever, thoughtful inside-forward but possibly came to Rangers just a trifle too late to do himself full justice. Kai Johansen became immortalised as the scorer of the winning goal in the 1966 Scottish Cup final replay against Celtic and for several years he gave classical displays at right-back. A good bit later, in the time of Graeme Souness, Jan Bartram shaped reasonably well in the number three shirt before having a public difference of opinion with his manager. For a time, the Danish connection was broken, but in the summer of 1994 Brian Laudrup has acquired instant popularity.

A forward who was more successful was the Swede, Orjan Persson, signed directly from Swedish football and whose direct style and fierce shooting seemed somehow more in the British than the Continental tradition. Twenty years later his fellow countryman Robert Prytz would arrive from Malmo and many Rangers supporters of that period thought that the side played its best football when both Prytz and Bobby Russell appeared together in the team.

Germany provided a goalkeeper in the person of Gerry Neef who in his time at Ibrox made many fine saves but conceded a few soft goals in crucial matches. He had previously been on trial with Aberdeen.

The most exotic arrivals were probably the two Russians, more precisely Ukranians, Oleg Kuznetzov and Alexi Mikhailichenko. The former was clearly a gifted player but gave the impression of finding the Premier Division over-hectic, and who is to say he was wrong. It is possible that this has applied also to Mikhailichenko but he was certainly worth selection for the big European games and he did many fine things in the great run of 1992-93. Every so often letters come in about what he said on being congratulated on a Scottish Cup Final win and what he actually said to the interviewer was, "I am very beautiful today".

Holland's representative was the colt-legged Peter Huistra, a player the supporters clearly found hard to fathom, judging by my letters. He had great qualities, in particular that of being able to pull crosses back and out, thus getting defences on the turn, but he often drifted out of a game and his relaxed approach could be taken, wrongly, for an over-casual attitude. He is perhaps too thoughtful for the frenzied, physical Scottish game.

For reasons of convenience, and because Israel has played in the European zone of international competitions, we may mention the two Israelis here. Bonni Ginzburg is dealt with elsewhere but he had a few good games in goal before Andy Goram made it clear that there was only one applicant for the job. Ari Cohen demonstrated that our own players had something to learn from his composed artistry. It may be that before too long there will be letters about the first Italian, Greek or Hungarian player to turn out for Rangers, for in football these days the net has to be cast ever wider.

FOREIGN PLAYERS

MONACO (Paisley) Where was Carl Hansen of Rangers playing when his leg was broken? Was it in a first-team game or was it in the reserves?

Hansen's leg was broken in a reserve team match against St Mirren at Love Street on February 23, 1924. He did not play again for Rangers after this accident.

KAZ (Bellshill) Apart from Johannes Edvaldsson, how many Icelandic players have appeared in Scottish football?

Only others I know of are Albert Gudmundsson who turned out for Rangers reserves during the Second World War and Thorolf (Tottie) Beck who had spells with St Mirren and Rangers in the 1960s.

RED ELVAN (Paisley) Did Gerry Neef go directly to Rangers from Germany or had he been with Aberdeen?

When Rangers signed him in August 1968, he had been on trial for a period with Aberdeen.

KENZIE (Springboig) Did Rangers have an Egyptian player before World War Two? I think his name was Mohammed Latif and I don't think he wore boots.

In the middle 1930s this player had a couple of seasons at Ibrox and he played once for the first team in a 1-1 draw with Hibernian at Easter Road in season 1933-34. He wore regulation footwear.

FAT FRED (Carmyle) I say that Rangers in the last 29 years have had a Danish, a German and an Israeli goalkeeper.

It might be just a shade longer than you suggest but certainly in the last 30 years Erik Sorensen, Gerhard Neef and Bonni Ginzburg respectively would meet these conditions.

COSO (Airdrie) Apart from Orjan Persson have Rangers ever had a Swedish player?

In the mid 1980s they had Robert Prytz who had come from the Swedish club Malmo.

THE SHIPPER (Duntocher) Have Rangers among their foreign players ever had an Italian or a Spanish player?

Not that I can recollect. Their foreign players have tended to come from Scandinavia, from Germany and from Russia. Now that you mention it it is odd that to all intents and purposes no players from these countries have made any impact on Scottish football as a whole.

J. Q. B. (Irvine) Of the present Rangers side of 1994 how many of them have had experience of French football?

Off the cuff I would say two and these would be Trevor Steven and Mark Hateley.

CHAPTER FIFTEEN

The Last Lines

When I took over the column way back in 1972 queries were still coming in about the early Ibrox goalkeepers such as Harry Rennie, Herbert Lock and Tom Hamilton. These have tended to slacken off and vanish with the years and even Jerry Dawson, that most elegant of keepers is moving into history. Occasionally the lesser lights will crop up, such as George Jenkins who valiantly understudied Jerry Dawson for a full ten years and a comparative handful of appearances for Dawson was only ever out through injury. There was John Shaw who filled the gap for a year between the departure of Jerry Dawson to Falkirk and the arrival of Bobby Brown from Queen's Park. Bobby Brown survived a traumatic first few months (not the only Rangers keeper to do that) and although some supporters considered him flashy and the rest of the defence resented his being paid several times what they were getting, he went on to become an eminently sound keeper who but for Willie Miller of Celtic and Jimmy Cowan of Morton would have won many more caps.

If Bobby Brown, although sound in method was occasionally inclined to the spectacular, the same could hardly be said of the

next two keepers, George Niven and Billy Ritchie. George was perhaps too undemonstrative for his own good. Particularly brave, he kept goal with the minimum of fuss and Billy Ritchie was no more flamboyant, although taller. Both went as by conveyor belt to Partick Thistle when their Ibrox stint was done.

Norrie Martin is a topic for questions because of the two horrendous injuries he sustained (fractured skull on two separate occasions) before making the first-team berth his own but it is with the coming of Gerhard Neef that the questions take off. He was not the first foreign keeper to play on a regular basis with Rangers, Erik Sorensen had come in 1968 and it is really remarkable how many non-Scottish goalkeepers have been given the Ibrox sweater since then.

It was a Scot who set the record for durability between the posts, namely Peter McCloy, son of a keeper although Peter's lad, the third generation in league football, is an outfield player with Kilmarnock. Many readers want to know who Peter McCloy saw off during his time at Ibrox in the course of his 16 years.

A couple of Scottish keepers then came and went comparatively quickly, Jim Stewart and Stewart Kennedy while Nicky Walker promised much on first arriving from Motherwell.

I have kept another myth for this section as it fits more easily here. There are still fans who insist that Rangers in the early 1990s had three international goalkeepers on their books at the same time, namely Chris Woods of England, Bonni Ginzburg of Israel and Andy Goram of Scotland, although also born in England. Once again this did not happen, Ginzburg had gone before the arrival of Goram and in fact Woods was off only a few months later.

Who was the best? The readers can't agree. It tends to be a question of age. Dawson is the choice of the older brigade but the

Opposite
Andy Goram of Rangers and Scotland. His superlative form in season 1992-93 had much to do with Rangers fine showing in Europe.

present-day fan cannot see anyone but Andy Goram and on his performance in the Champions Cup in 1993 it would be hard to argue. I take refuge in the fact that the column is a record of fact, rather than opinion and there is reason to think that had he been given the chance Jerry Dawson would have acquitted himself extremely well in serious European competition.

GOALKEEPERS

JOHN B. (Alloa) When did George Niven sign for Rangers and when did he make his debut in the first team?

George Niven came to Rangers from Couper Angus Juniors in 1947 but did not play in the first team until the last game of season 1951-52.

ODDITY (Carnwadric) I maintain that Rangers had a goalkeeper just after the Second World War who was signed from Queen's Park as an inside-forward.

Correct. Archie McIndewar was signed from Queen's Park as an inside-forward but for season 1947-48 he was listed as Bobby Brown's understudy.

A. HERD (Lambhill) What was the record of Rangers' goalkeeper Tom Sinclair while on loan to Celtic in 1906?

Excellent, in fact it could not have been better. In eight matches which he played Tom Sinclair did not concede a goal and he actually won a Glasgow Cup medal. It was a saner game in those days.

Calling J. DONALD (Castlemilk)

Thank you for your reminder that Rangers' signing of goalkeeper John Shaw during season 1944-45 was prompted at least in part by serious injuries to Jerry Dawson and the reserve goalkeeper George Jenkins.

A. W. (Milton) Did goalkeeper John Shaw not take over from Jerry Dawson before the arrival of Bobby Brown?

Yes, Jerry Dawson had his last game for Rangers in November 1945 and from then until the end of the season Shaw was the first-choice goalkeeper until the coming of Bobby Brown from Queen's Park in May 1946.

TOPICAL TIMES (Glasgow) Who were the regular Old Firm keepers before Tom Hamilton of Rangers and Peter Shevlin of Celtic?

I would say that Willie Robb for Rangers and Charlie Shaw with Celtic would be the men you are after.

BRUCE ROAD (London) How many Rangers goalkeepers have gone on to play for Partick Thistle?

I can think of at least two and these would be George Niven and Billy Ritchie who both had a spell at Firhill when their Ibrox days were done. The trail from Ibrox to Firhill was a well-worn one with Torry Gillick taking it as a player, Arthur Dixon as a trainer and Willie Thornton and Davie Meiklejohn as managers.

JOCK THE LODGER (Hamilton) Who were the Rangers goalkeepers during the Second World War?

Broken only by injury they were Jerry Dawson in the first team and George Jenkins in the reserves.

CHAPTER SIXTEEN

South African Players

Rangers have had a long-standing connection with South Africa, going back to the arrival of Billy Arnison right at the end of the Second World War. He only played a handful of games for the first team but in them he averaged almost a goal a game. One important match in which he played was the last of the Southern League Cup Finals in 1946 when Rangers went down 3-2 to Aberdeen. A few years later another player bearing the name Arnison, Neil this time, had a few games for Rangers between 1955 and 1957 and the number of his goals, 3, was only one less than the number of his games, 4, so it seems that he might well have been worth a longer try.

A frequent source of questions is another South African Johnny Hubbard, with whom I had the great pleasure of playing in an Air Force side for almost a full season. He was small and slight, nine stone dripping wet in the old phrase and he was a very accomplished all-round sportsman. He had one remarkable peculiarity. Highly ambidextrous, he was right-handed in those games which he played one-handed, e.g. tennis and badminton, and left-handed in those games that required both hands, e.g. cricket and snooker.

He was also almost certainly the best taker of a penalty kick the game has ever seen. I used to be at the sharp end in goal as he practised against me. A leisurely approach, a swivel of the body and the ball was on its way quite slowly along the ground as you, the keeper, set off in the other direction. He got you to shift your weight the wrong way, that was all. Naturally most of the questions about him relate to penalties as he went almost seven years without missing one.

Nothing like as subtle a player, although extremely useful, was Don Kichenbrand, big and rumbustious, curiously like a predecessor of his at Ibrox, Jimmy Smith. He had the same urge to shoulder goalkeepers over the line, usually fairly, and although incredibly clumsy-looking at times he had the capacity to bring off the most unexpectedly delicate touches and flicks. He was at Ibrox for only three seasons and of his 29 League appearances all but four were made in his first season, 1955-56. Yet he was so unusual a player that his memory remains very vivid with those who saw him and his nickname, 'the Rhino', described him well.

At that time many Scottish clubs had South African players, Dundee, Aberdeen and Clyde in particular while in England Charlton Athletic were a noted Springbok outpost. This led to a famous match at Ibrox in March 1956 when Scotland played a UK-based South African side. For once in a way the majority of the crowd supported South Africa, given that Kichenbrand and Hubbard were both in the South African side.

After Kichenbrand there was a long gap until, at the second time of asking and a few years late, Richard Gough became the last player to date from that country to join up at Ibrox.

SOUTH AFRICA

GRAHAM'S (Glasgow) Who was in goal for Celtic when Johnny Hubbard scored a hat-trick for Rangers on New Year's Day 1955?

Andy Bell from Arthurlie was in goal deputising for John Bonnar.

JACK (Ayr) Where did Johnny Hubbard of Rangers have his last game in British football?

Leaving Rangers in 1959 Hubbard had three seasons with Bury, joined Ayr United in June 1962 and got a free transfer in April 1964. I cannot find him playing senior after that.

BIG ANDY (Glasgow) How long was Johnny Hubbard at Ibrox before he played for the first team?

He joined Rangers in July 1949 and had his first game for the league team against Partick Thistle at Ibrox on September 10 of that year.

BIG DAVIE (Renfrew) Was Don Kichenbrand ever in direct opposition to Jock Stein in club games?

The two men were in opposition in two Old Firm games in season 1955-56.

BILL WILSON (Cathcart) Some time ago Scotland played a South African XI at Ibrox. Please give the teams, score and status of the fixture.

Scotland beat South Africa 2-1 at Ibrox on March 12, 1956 in a match which was used as an international trial.

Teams were,

SCOTLAND, Younger (Hibernian), Parker, Rae, (both Falkirk), Evans (Celtic), Malloy (Cardiff City), Glen (Aberdeen), Smith (Hibernian), McMillan (Airdrieonians), Reilly (Hibernian), Collins (Celtic), Mitchell (Newcastle United).

SOUTH AFRICA, Rudham (Liverpool), O'Linn, Hewie, (both Charlton Athletic), Purdon (Sunderland), Neilson (Bury), Chamberlain (Charlton Athletic), Davies (Luton), Leary (Charlton Athletic), Kichenbrand (Rangers), Foreman (Brighton), Hubbard (Rangers).

Scorers were Reilly and Collins for Scotland and Hubbard, pen. for South Africa. The attendance was 54,000.

THORN INN (Johnstone) When did Don Kichenbrand arrive at Ibrox and when did he leave?

Coming from Delfos in 1955 Don was at Ibrox until November 1957 when he moved to Sunderland and the following season he was the English side's top scorer with 21 league goals.

DEADSHOT (Bowling) Who were the only three goalkeepers to save penalty kicks taken by Johnny Hubbard of Rangers in first-team matches?

In order they were Dave Walker of Airdrie, Jimmy Brown of Kilmarnock and Bert Slater of Falkirk. Hubbard's miss at Broomfield was his first in 23 attempts.

CHAPTER SEVENTEEN

What the Readers Wanted to be Told Happened – But Didn't

On both sides of the Old Firm there are fondly cherished myths which would have been nice had they happened but they did not. It is, however, hard to convince readers of this and no matter how many denials one puts in the column the questions on a particular topic continue to come.

For instance, around the late 1920s and early 1930s, Rangers had three players on their books called Hamilton. There was Tom, the goalkeeper who made a dramatic save in the 1928 Scottish Cup Final when the match was still goalless, and defenders Jimmy and Bob Hamilton, the last an Ulsterman who was always known as Newry Hamilton from his place of origin.

What the fans want is a Rangers first team with these three in it but although it would have been possible it never in fact happened, not at least in a first-team competitive match. Had it done so there was every chance that in an Old Firm match they would have come up against the three Thomsons of Celtic, John in goal and the forwards Alex and Bertie. But although that would certainly have been highly unusual it remains a might-have-been.

Also on names there was a deluge of correspondence in the mid-1980s trying to establish that Rangers had played a side whose surnames all ended in the letter n. It seems incredible that this did not happen around 1970 when a study of the list of signed players revealed 16 with such a name but captain and manager John Greig was the fellow who stopped this happening.

Dale Gordon celebrates after scoring against Motherwell in November 1991. This clever player followed the trail blazed by Mohammed Latif and Mark Walters.

CHAPTER EIGHTEEN

Rangers,
the First Coloured Player

Many Rangers supporters believe that Mark Walters was the first coloured player to play for Rangers, soon to be followed by Dale Gordon. But this had in fact already happened many years before. In the mid-1930s Mohammed Latif, an Egyptian student attending the School of Physical Education at Jordanhill College had a couple of season with Rangers Reserves playing in what was then called the Alliance. He was a fairly regular contender in season 1934-35 when he scored seven goals in 16 games for the "stiffs" and he made a few appearances in the two following seasons. He actually turned out in a first-team league match against Hibernian at Easter Road and also in that side was Bob McPhail, the oldest-surviving Scottish internationalist and the oldest Rangers player.

Later on Mohammed Latif became head of television sports broadcasting in Egypt and was a well-known figure at successive World Cups. He must have enjoyed his time in Glasgow for as a result of his recommendation Mustapha Mansour, who was also a student at Jordanhill College from 1937-1939 gave Queen's Park two excellent years of service as a goalkeeper. It will be seen therefore that the connection of non-European players with Scottish football goes back a considerable way.

CHAPTER NINETEEN

The Scapegoats

In the history of any club which has been in existence for over a century, there will be a few players whom the supporters regard as having been treated badly, sacrificed for a bad performance on an important day. The most spectacular instances of this would be George McLean and Jim Forrest, axed from first team responsibility after the shock defeat at Berwick in the Scottish Cup in January 1967.

The support felt then that it was wrong to take this defeat out on two forwards who had been prolific scorers in their time at Ibrox and indeed continued to be so with their new clubs. Jim Forrest in particular was to live to score quite a few goals against Rangers when he came back from England to join Aberdeen. George McLean had the truly astonishing strike rate of two goals every three games in a Rangers career which extended over more than 100 games. Robert McElroy of the *Rangers Historian* makes the incontestable point that if Rangers had retained these two players in the front line until the end of that season, they might very well have won the Cup Winners Cup five years before they did, bearing in mind the makeshift forward line that took the field against Bayern Munich in 1967.

Occasionally a defender suffered in this way, John Valentine disappearing for all practical purposes after the 7-1 League Cup Final defeat of 1957. It would be wrong to say that there was anything like as much public sympathy for Valentine. It was a

Cup Final after all and the opponents were Celtic. But he was perhaps entitled to reflect that he did not receive anything like the support from his wing-halves that he might reasonably have expected.

Occasionally players can survive the truly horrendous match. In the first Old Firm game at Ibrox in season 1993-94 Alistair Maxwell lost two very bad late goals which cost the match. It would have been the easy and popular thing to do to drop the keeper but Walter Smith stuck by him and Maxwell went on to play some fine games in goal before the eventual return of Andy Goram. Another, Alistair McCoist, survived a long period of managerial disfavour under Graeme Souness to become one of the outstanding strikers in the Scottish game. He of all people is bound to have a soft spot for Jim Forrest and George McLean.

CHAPTER TWENTY

The Greatest Friendly Match of All

Nowadays friendly matches against foreign sides are part of the normal calendar and are inevitably a bit devalued by their very frequency. Perhaps that is why the friendly match which continues all these years to draw the most correspondence is the famous game against Moscow Dynamo in the autumn of 1945.

The love affair with Russia was turning sour even six months after the end of the war. The Dynamo side had carried all before them on their tour of Britain, drawing with Chelsea, annihilating Cardiff City, defeating Arsenal and complaining bitterly about the large number of guest players Arsenal had used.

They made it clear that if they came up to Glasgow they would play a club side, not a disguised national side. Before a ball was kicked the Russians threatened to go back south if Jimmy Caskie played for Rangers. They could not be persuaded that Rangers were actually negotiating a permanent transfer of Caskie from Hibernian and that he would not appear as simply a guest player.

The Russians were adamant and rather than prejudice the match Rangers yielded. There were almost 100,000 in the ground when the Russians ran out in their strange, wide, baggy shorts with a coloured circle round the bottom of each leg. Half a million people will tell you that they were there but I was. I was one of the thousands of schoolboys who were marked missing that day and later when I was a headmaster I always felt sympathy for lads in similar case although officially one had to deplore their action.

With 24 minutes of the match gone the truants wished they had gone to school. The Russians were two up, one a well-worked goal, the other a free kick that Jerry Dawson in his last big-game appearance for Rangers seemed to be distinctly slow in diving for. Gradually Rangers hauled themselves into the match and got a clear-cut penalty. Waddell took it and the famous keeper Tiger Khomich touched it over the bar. Just before half-time Rangers gave themselves a lifeline when Jimmy Smith scrambled an inelegant but priceless goal.

In the second-half Dynamo tired under the weight of tour games and more importantly the relentless Rangers pressure as the other Tiger, Shaw, and George Young drove their team-mates on. A Russian sub came on but nobody went off and for five minutes it was, "Come away the twelve men".

Still the Russian defence held out though by now never threatening to score again and it seemed as if Rangers might be thwarted. With a few minutes to go there was a half-hearted claim for a Rangers penalty. The referee rejected it but his attention was drawn to the stand side linesman Bobby Calder, later a well-known referee and scout for Aberdeen. He stood with flag raised and after consultation a penalty was given. I have to say I thought it soft then and do now, whereas the first penalty was in the old phrase "stonewall". Not unnaturally Willie Waddell was not breaking his neck to take this one and it was left to big George Young. With tremendous calm he sent a waist-high shot past Khomich and a few minutes later the whistle sounded.

Rangers had got a very honourable draw but the more far-seeing fans were not deceived. It was clear that the great side which had dominated Scottish war-time football was all of a sudden much too old. Changes would be needed and they were made. What was equally clear was that European football had suddenly moved to a new dimension. No longer could we regard it as something interesting but faintly comic, "Clever chaps, but they can't shoot, you know". They could and they did. It was a thoughtful crowd that spilled out along Copland Road into the autumn night.

RANGERS v MOSCOW DYNAMO 1945

BRIG BAR (Easterhouse) **What were the admission prices for the match between Rangers and Moscow Dynamo at Ibrox in 1945?**

Prices were two guineas, one guinea, 15/6, 10 shillings and 5 shillings for the stand, 3/6 for the enclosure and 2/6 (12.5 p) for the terracing.

WEE McCANN (Govanhill) **In the Story of Rangers I think the author errs in naming the Moscow Dynamo right back against Rangers at Ibrox in 1945. I say the three defenders were Khomich, Cherniansky and Stankeveitch.**

The Moscow Dynamo team given was Khomich, Radikorsky and Stankevitch (note spelling).

HAIL THE PIRATES (Wishaw) **I read that when Moscow Dynamo played Arsenal the Russians protested because they were playing a select side. How many genuine Arsenal players were there in the team?**

The Russians had a point. Of the Arsenal side which lost 4-3 only five men, Scott, Bastin, Joy, Drury and Cumnor were actually on Arsenal's books. The Highbury side included as guests Matthews of Stoke City, Mortensen of Blackpool and Bacuzzi and Rooke of Fulham.

J. R. (Cardonald) **My friend maintains that Dougie Gray played at right-back against Moscow Dynamo but I say it was David Gray. Who is right?**

You are, it was David who was at right-back in the 2-2 draw in November 1945.

PHILIP THE FAN (Carntyne) **Teams and scorers in the Rangers v Moscow Dynamo game of 1945 please.**

Teams were, RANGERS, Dawson, David Gray, Shaw, Watkins, Young, Symon, Waddell, Gillick, Smith, Williamson, Johnstone.

MOSCOW DYNAMO, Khomich, Radikorsky, Stankevich, Blinkov, Semichastny, Oreshkin, Archangelsky, Karsev, Beskov, Bobrov, Soloviev.

The referee was T Thompson of Leamington. Karsev scored twice for Dynamo before Smith and Young, pen. brought Rangers level. Earlier Waddell had missed a penalty and Duncanson came on as a second-half substitute.

THE HOOK (Partick) Apart from Rangers what other teams did Moscow Dynamo play on their 1945 tour of Britain?

They drew 3-3 with Chelsea and then beat Cardiff City 10-1 and Arsenal 4-3 in a match played in impenetrable fog.

SASHA (Maryhill) Was the Rangers v Moscow Dynamo match in 1945 played in thick fog?

No. It looked threatening in the morning but the weather cleared a bit around midday although it remained misty.

CHAPTER TWENTY-ONE

The Managers

It is not only the players who are the subject of the Now You Know enquiries. There is a constant stream of requests for information on the managers. It is reasonable to take William Struth as the first manager of Rangers in the modern sense. His predecessor, William Wilton, the unfortunate victim of a drowning accident in 1920 could be more accurately described as secretary-manager, a description which would also have fitted those who had gone before him.

WILLIAM STRUTH

Struth remains a mysterious figure, aloof and dominating. His early background was in athletics rather than football. Indeed he came to prominence as an athlete and trainer in athletics. It was for this that he was recommended to Clyde and thereafter to Rangers. It was this background which gave him his lifelong interest in track and field events and led him to make the Rangers Sports the leading athletic meeting in the British calendar, the only possible rival being the Amateur Athletic Association meeting

Opposite
Bill Struth – for more than 30 yearts he guided the destiny of Rangers and did more than anyone until that time to make them a pre-eminent British club

and even there the Rangers Sports very often had the more distinguished guest list. The Sports themselves attract quite a few questions from older readers, not surprising when one recalls that such immortals as Paavo Nurmi, Sydney Wooderson, McDonald Bailey and our own Alan Paterson performed with distinction at Ibrox.

A potted impression of Bill Struth might be – "Distinguished-looking, always immaculately turned-out (he kept a separate wardrobe at Ibrox and would frequently change outfits in the course of the day) didn't bother much with the detail of tactics". This was not absolutely true, I remember Jerry Dawson saying something which indicated that few things escaped Struth's notice. In Jerry's own words:

"I had arrived at Ibrox just before the rule was changed which allowed a goalkeeper to tap the ball to a colleague inside the penalty area and then collect his pass-back. From now on the ball had to clear the penalty box from a goal-kick. One day at training Bill Struth came to me and said, "I have been watching you for some time Dawson, and you are a very poor kicker of a dead ball. You will never be a good one but you have two weeks to become an adequate one." With that he turned on his heel and walked back up the tunnel. I had come to Ibrox from Camelon Labour Exchange and if I did not make it I was going back to Camelon Labour Exchange. I tell you Bob, *that*'s pressure." (We had been talking about pressure in the modern game.)

Struth was very methodical. I have a copy of his training regulations which Jerry Dawson gave me. Among the Do's and Don'ts, "Don't swim in fresh water, cycle or play badminton in the playing season." On the positive side, strips had to be immaculate. He once sent a player back to change before a pre-season trial on noticing that his studs had caught one leg of his shorts and left a dirty mark. The players had strict instructions to run out of the tunnel at half-time even if three goals down, not something that happened with great frequency in Struth's time.

How good was he? He certainly built up an unchallenged League supremacy between the two wars and although Hibernian menaced with their three wins after 1945 Rangers were getting back on course when he handed over to Scot Symon in 1954. There was of course no competitive European football in his day so although readers want to do this, it is hard to place him in perspective. There is no reason to think that he could not have adapted to this challenge, after all in the great series of friendlies with Arsenal, which were certainly played in a competitive spirit, Rangers fully held their own.

His overwhelming preference in the first-team was for a squad of approximately 15 players, especially in his latter years, and rather than bring in the designated reserve, he relied very heavily on utility men such as Willie Rae or Willie Findlay even if that meant three or four positional changes. He more than anyone established Rangers as a top-flight British club and perhaps his last major service to them was to take war-time football seriously between 1939-45 so that Rangers were well-placed for the resumption of normal competition .

JAMES SCOTLAND SYMON

By 1954 it was clear that increasing age and failing health was bringing Bill Struth's remarkable tenure of office to a close. His chosen successor was a former player, Scot Symon, who had been on the Ibrox books from 1938 until 1947, therefore inevitably playing most of his time in wartime football. Before coming to Rangers he had served Dundee and Portsmouth and it is fair to say that he was a good but not outstanding player. A tough-tackling wing-half he had but the one cap, against Hungary in 1938.

Right from the start he had shown evidence of unusual managerial skills with different clubs (in this respect there is a startling parallel with the career of Jock Stein). Starting with unfashionable East Fife he won an incredible three League Cups with them, once when they were still a Second Division side. He also won the Second Division championship and reached a

A royal occasion – Rangers manager Scot Symon greets HRH Princess Margaret and the Earl of Snowdon on a visit to Ibrox. Rangers chairman John Lawrence is in the centre

Scottish Cup Final before losing to Rangers as it happened. Economics meant that he could not keep his star players at Methil and he himself joined the trek south to become manager of Preston North End. He was there one brief year but took his side to the FA Cup Final where he only lost out by virtue of a last-minute penalty to West Bromwich Albion.

He had therefore the ideal background to succeed Struth with the additional advantage of comparative youth and a realisation that from now on Europe would be the place where the really big battles would be fought.

He was basically a reserved man who gave the appearance of finding it difficult to relax. The most famous though possibly invented quote about him was of a reporter phoning up on the very foggy afternoon of one of the early European ties at Ibrox to ascertain weather conditions at the ground to be met by the Symon response – "I don't know, and don't quote me." Everyone knew it was the sort of thing he was liable to say.

It is strange that questions about this most formal of men tend to be about oddities. He is the only Rangers manager to have played a full match for the club in goal. He remains to this day the Scot with the best bowling analysis against an Australian Test side and has an honoured place in *Wisden*, the cricketer's Bible.

Europe was a difficult field in which to operate. There were the successes of twice reaching the final of the Cup Winners Cup but there were also some thrashings suffered along the way. Some very astute signings, Jim Baxter and Ian McMillan notable among them, secured almost total domination of Scottish football in the early 1960s when only Hearts and briefly Dundee threatened Ibrox supremacy.

This changed of course with the arrival of Stein at Parkhead. Defeat by Celtic is always more difficult to take than any other adverse result and although the Cup win of 1966 over the old enemy had appeared to stem the tide of Celtic successes this proved to be the falsest of dawns. Defeat at Berwick the following year and the over-hasty jettisoning of Forest and McLean meant that Rangers had no forwards worth the name for the Cup Winners final in Nuremberg and a less than world-beating Bayern Munich side got away with a 1-0 win in extra time.

When an indifferent start was made to season 1967-68 Symon's days were numbered. If the decision to change the pilot was right, and a case could be made for it, the manner of carrying it out gave great offence and created a widespread feeling that a notable club servant had been shabbily treated. His dismissal was indirectly conveyed to him by an intermediary.

He recovered his spirits at least partially and became first manager and then general manager of Partick Thistle. I get letters about that too! The remainder of his career was in truth something of an anti-climax.

I have happy personal memories of Scot Symon, perhaps because we shared a passionate attachment to cricket. In his Partick Thistle days he learned that I was giving a course on The History and Economics of Scottish Football at Glasgow University and expressed a wish to come. He attended all 10 lectures and was kind enough to say he had found them enjoyable and instructive. In all my time in football I have never had a greater compliment.

DAVID WHITE

Perhaps because of his comparatively short spell in office, some two years, David White does not attract so many questions although some readers are interested in his playing career (he was a very good wing-half with Clyde) before he came to Rangers as assistant manager.

There are others not slow to point out that he had a remarkably good record against Celtic but the latter club were at the height of their powers then and David White would have needed to regain the league title to stay in the job. As it was he went in November 1969 after a home and away defeat from the Polish side Gornik in the Cup Winners Cup. He was undoubtedly unfortunate in the

Davie White took over the managership from Scot Symon but his tenure of office was caomparatively brief

timing of his appointment although even at the outset there had been those who felt that someone was needed with a longer experience of the club. That person now stood in the wings.

WILLIE WADDELL

Now You Know could almost have been kept going on this man alone. Indeed it was only in answering the many questions on Willie Waddell that one came to realise what a remarkable career his had been. He burst into fame in 1938 by appearing in every sense "out of the blue" against Arsenal and he was to play at top level for eighteen years. For many of those years he was an automatic selection at outside-right for Scotland and this at a time when such men as Gordon Smith of Hibernian and Jimmy Delaney of Celtic were also available. He won every domestic honour and his partnership with Torry Gillick was in the line of the great Scottish partnerships such as Stevenson and Ferrier of Motherwell. He had eight highly successful years as Kilmarnock manager, finishing second several times and eventually leading them to the title in 1965 (he remains the only Rangers manager to have led another Scottish team to a First Division championship.) He was in charge for Rangers greatest-ever success, the Cup Winners triumph against Moscow Dynamo in Barcelona in 1972 but immediately afterwards moved upstairs to become General Manager.

Before that he had undergone the trauma of the Ibrox Disaster of January 1971 and had dedicated himself to the building of the new Ibrox which took shape over the next twenty years. He rounded off his full tour of duty from apprentice to director by joining the Board in 1973 and eventually filling the position of vice-chairman. For part of his career, he had somehow managed to find the time to become an extremely competent journalist. It is a measure of his contribution that the first questions from readers link him with Bob McPhail and Alec Venters, both early team-

mates of his, and by the end of his time at Ibrox as a director he
had seen the new stadium pass from plan to building to occupation.

*Willie Waddell, distinguished as player, manager and general manager and the
driving force behind the new Ibrox Stadium*

JOCK WALLACE

It fell to Jock Wallace to be associated with Rangers blackest day in the playing sense, the Scottish Cup defeat at Berwick in 1967 when he did more than anyone to bring about the upset, and also some of their greatest triumphs such as the two Trebles which the club recorded in their first spell with him in charge.

It was very noticeable that Wallace inspired great affection. His fierce training methods were legendary, born of his own rigorous army experience – several readers clearly believed he had eaten monkeys while in the jungles of Malaya!

His great strength was the ability to instil confidence into his players and to build a tremendous rapport with the fans. This was never better demonstrated than in the late autumn of 1993 when, visibly ailing, he appeared at Ibrox before an important Old Firm match to receive a prolonged ovation from the home support and, from the evidence of my own eyes, quite a few visitors too. He left Ibrox abruptly first-time round in circumstances that remain mysterious but after spells with Leicester City and Motherwell he was prevailed upon to take charge for a second term at Ibrox. Again he gave everything he had, although it would be wrong to say that this term was anything like as successful. For most of his second spell he had to contend not only with a temporarily revived Celtic but with the New Firm of Aberdeen and Dundee United who actually posed the greater threat.

He certainly possessed the common touch, witness his bringing on the long-term injured John Greig for the last few minutes at Easter Road so that the player who had fought hardest in the dark days could be in at the death when the championship was at last regained. There are people in football who are admired, however reluctantly, by the opposition and Jock Wallace is certainly one of them.

Opposite
Jock Wallace as he prepares to take over the managerial reins for the second time in November 1983

now you know *about* . . . RANGERS

JOHN GREIG

The overwhelming bulk of questions about John Greig relate to his playing days. It is not that he knew no success as a manager – although missing out on the major prize, in a five year spell he won two League Cups and two Scottish Cups – but rather that his playing career was so extraordinary. It lasted 18 years, only Dougie Gray made more than his 857 first-appearance and Gray played four years longer. The honours list is endless, Player of the Year on two separate occasions, five League Championships, six Scottish Cups and three League Cups in addition to 44 caps and a European Cup Winners Cup medal.

Many past Rangers players could show something approaching as impressive a list of awards won. What set John Greig aside and gave him a unique place in the hearts of supporters was his tremendous defiance during the bad years of the mid and late Sixties and the early Seventies. There were matches during that time when the impression given was that John Greig was playing the opposition on his own.

After leaving Ibrox he became a very successful radio broadcaster but he welcomed the invitation to return to the club as Public Relations Officer in which capacity he has also succeeded admirably. As a manager he had the misfortune to encounter Aberdeen and Dundee United at their best at a time when the Ibrox playing staff was, to be charitable, in a transitional stage and the rebuilding of the stadium was the top priority. The affection in which he was held was never better demonstrated than by the enormous success of his testimonial match when at last he decided to stop playing.

Opposite
Player becomes boss – John Greig answers a call of congratulations on his first day in the managerial seat at Ibrox

GRAEME SOUNESS

As has happened all through his career, Graeme Souness can be relied upon to arouse conflicting emotions in the Now You Know column. On the one hand there is gratitude for his having turned the club round and this he undoubtedly did with three championships in his first four years there and another almost in the bag when he shocked the fans by his decision to move to manage Liverpool. This was by many seen as a betrayal, however naively, and there were those too who had never taken to his abrasive style of managership and the adverse publicity which this constantly earned for the club. His assets were many, it must be said. He had a profound knowledge of the English game, who was good and more important, who might become available. It is indisputable that Rangers successes under Souness and thereafter Walter Smith owed much to the English contingent. He shuffled players in and out of Ibrox as by a revolving door and many questions deal with the sheer volume of signings. One of his great strengths as a manager was the ability to recognise that a signing would not fit in and therefore would have to be moved on quickly, which he almost always did at a profit.

The manager was however a turbulent spirit who seemed to court controversy and this led to fall-outs with his own players, notably Terry Butcher. It was nevertheless a tremendous shock when Souness decided to head south with a vital game against Aberdeen still to be played. Rangers having won on the last day 2-0, Souness phoned up to see how his team had done and on receiving the enquiry, "Your team?" growled sardonically, "They would have been my team if they had lost." His great contribution to Rangers was to re-instil a sense of self-belief which he reinforced by making Rangers attractive to top English players, thus reversing the transfer trail which had bedevilled Scottish football for so long.

Opposite
What'll it be like at the end? – Graeme Souness on the first day of his appointment as player-manager

WALTER SMITH

To date there have been comparatively few questions about Walter Smith but it has always been a feature of the column that when managers are succeeding they do not attract over-many questions. Even Jock Stein tended to attract more questions about his managership in latter days when he was less successful. Since Walter Smith has been eminently and almost unbrokenly successful to date this would explain the comparative quiet. There was a flurry of interest at the outset as many had expected another big name down South might be approached. The chairman David Murray had been sufficiently impressed and sufficiently courageous to give Smith his chance in full control. And in David Murray's own words it was "one of the best decisions I ever made".

It is one thing to have unlimited money available, another to use it wisely, as other clubs have learned before now. The new format of the European Cup makes immediate comparisons with past achievements difficult but Smith's modest acceptance of the club's fine performance on the Continent in 1992-93 and his philosophical recognition of the huge disappointment of 1993-94 have confirmed him as one of the leading British managers and in years to come the letters will flood in to have his achievements confirmed and his ability recognised. Now in the early autumn of 1994 he faces his biggest test to date as the first team he created shows signs of the need for a major reconstruction.

Opposite
Will it be a cricket score? – manager Walter Smith is in thoughtful mood as he supervises training at the ground of Clydesdale Cricket Club

THE RANGERS MANAGERS
ON-FIELD AND OFF

BLUE NOSES (Glasgow) How many players did David White sign for Rangers while he was manager?

In addition to various young signings he brought back Jim Baxter from Nottingham Forest, signed Gerry Neef from Germany and arranged the transfers of Colin Stein and Alex MacDonald from Hibernian and St Johnstone respectively.

BLUE NOSE (Dalmarnock) If Scot Symon in an emergency kept goal for Rangers for a whole game against Clyde at Shawfield around 1941-42 can you oblige with the teams? I think Rangers scored eight goals

On April 6, 1942 Rangers beat Clyde 8-2.

Teams were,

CLYDE, Fraser, Wilson, Inglis, Deans, Blair, Winning, Agnew, Anderson, Wallace, Williams, Fitzsimmons.

RANGERS, Symon, Gray, Shaw, Bolt, Woodburn, Little, Waddell, Venters, McIntosh, Marshall, Johnston.

BLUE BOY (Tillicoultry) How many times were Rangers League champions and winners of the Scottish Cup, League Cup, Glasgow Cup and Charity Cup with Bill Struth as manager?

They won the league 18 times, the Scottish Cup 10 times, the League Cup twice, the Glasgow Cup 19 times and the Charity Cup 18 times. In addition there were several wartime successes.

PRECAST (Glasgow) Please give David White's position at Ibrox just before Scot Symon finished as manager.

David White was assistant manager at this time.

BIG CHA (Cambuslang) Am I correct in saying that John Greig played at inside-right against St Mirren and scored three goals?

On September 1, 1962 John Greig at inside-right scored three goals in a 4-0 League Cup victory over St Mirren. Jimmy Millar scored the other Ibrox goal.

BALLANTINE'S (Brightons) When Scot Symon was replaced by Davie White what position were Rangers in the league?

When David White took over in October 1967 Rangers were top of the league with 14 points, having played 8 matches.

Calling R. CRAIG (Glasgow)

I have now found the information you requested. Willie Waddell and Alex Scott appeared in the same Rangers team against Aberdeen at Pittodrie in 1955. They also played together in a friendly against Linfield in Belfast the following month.

D. D. D. (Stepps) What was Davie White's junior club before he signed for Clyde?

He went to Shawfield in 1957 from the Lanarkshire junior club Royal Albert.

CURIOUS (Springburn) For how many seasons were Jock Stein and Jock Wallace in direct opposition as managers? During that time which of them won most major honours – i. e. League, League Cup and Scottish Cup?

They were in competition from June 1972 until May 1978 and in that time each won three league championships. They also each won three Scottish Cups and Jock Wallace won two League Cups as opposed to Stein's one. The issue is slightly complicated by the fact that Sean Fallon was effectively in charge of Celtic for one of those seasons.

RIGGER (Whiteinch) Did Scot Symon ever win a full cap (not a war-time one) with Scotland? If so, how many other Rangers players were in the side?

Scot Symon was capped against Hungary in season 1938-39 when the Scotland goalkeeper was his club-mate Jerry Dawson.

RED DIAMOND (Airdrie) Please give date, attendance and Scotland side in the match against Rangers for John Greig's Testimonial match.

On April 16, 1978 65,000 saw this Scotland side lose by 5-0: Blyth (Coventry City), Brownlie (Hibernian), Whittaker (Partick Thistle), Masson (Derby County), McQueen (Manchester United), Rioch (Derby County), Robertson (Nottingham Forest), Wallace (Coventry City), Jordan (Manchester United), Hartford (Manchester City), Gemmell (Nottingham Forest).

ODDITY (Carnwadric) I am sure John Greig's last game as

manager was against a Motherwell side managed by Jock Wallace.

On October 22, 1983 Motherwell, managed by Jock Wallace, defeated Rangers 2-1 at Ibrox but John Greig was still in charge of Rangers in a League Cup tie against Hearts before his resignation was announced on October 28.

Calling EXILED MOULDER (Tunstall)

A few weeks ago I overlooked an example right under my nose. John Greig of course won a Scottish Cup medal as a player against Aberdeen in 1978 and then managed the Ibrox side to success in the final against Hibernian in the following season.

GLEN MARIE (Coatbridge) Who won the most leagues and cups as a manager, Scot Symon or Jock Stein?

Scot Symon took Rangers to six League successes, five Scottish Cups and four League Cups 15 major honours in all. Jock Stein had 10 League successes, eight Scottish Cups six League Cups and a European Cup, making a total of 25 major honours won.

THE LOANING (Kirkintilloch) When did John Greig sign for Rangers and when did he become their manager?

He went to Ibrox in 1960 from Whitburn Juniors and moved to the manager's office in May 1978.

DUMMY MOUSE (Pollokshields) What was Jock Wallace's record in European matches during his first spell at Ibrox?

He broke exactly even in competitive matches with five wins, five defeats and four draws.

ACE CLUB (Glasgow) Who has made the most appearances for Rangers?

I prefer to confine myself to league matches in these matters and on that score John Greig, with 496 matches would come top of the list at the time of writing in 1984.

PIGEON JAKE (Milton) How many goals did wingers Gordon Smith and Willie Waddell score in their careers and for how long did they play?

In a playing career lasting from 1938 until 1955 Willie Waddell scored 154 goals while Gordon Smith who played from 1941 until 1963 scored 306 goals. I have counted all competitive matches including wartime ones but not friendlies.

ANGORA (Baillieston) When Bill Struth came to Rangers had he any previous managerial experience?

No, he had been trainer with Clyde and of course first came to Rangers in that capacity.

CASTLE STREET (Glasgow) What clubs did Scot Symon play with before and after Rangers?

Before coming to Rangers in 1938 he had been with Dundee and Portsmouth but he did not play any football after leaving Ibrox, going off to manage East Fife.

COWGATE (Kirkintilloch) How many of Rangers managers have had managerial experience with English clubs?

Scot Symon managed Preston North End, Jock Wallace had a spell as manager of Leicester City and of course Graeme Souness was subsequently in charge of Liverpool.

MAXICARD (Neilston) Did Walter Smith play for any other Scottish senior club besides Dundee United?

He had a short spell with Dumbarton before rejoining Dundee United.

Calling BUDGIE FANCIER (Lennoxtown)

Willie Waddell and Scot Symon would be the only two Rangers managers ever to have played in the same Rangers team.

Chapter twenty-two

The Scottish Cup

It is a curious fact that although Rangers have been very successful in the Scottish Cup their success has tended to come in clusters. It is therefore hardly surprising that even almost 70 years on questions continue to come in on the final which ended the longest drought of all, that of 1928 when in beating Celtic 4-0 at Hampden, Rangers ended a gap of 25 years since their last success.

In one sense the gap was not as long as it appears, since of course there was no official Cup competition between 1915 and 1919 inclusive. But it was a long wait, made all the more joyful at the end by the victory over the club's greatest rivals. It started a period of prolific Cup winning. There was only one national cup in those days, and although Rangers lost in the final the following year, Partick Thistle were beaten in 1930 and Kilmarnock in 1932, both at the second attempt, before the treble of 1934-36, a curiosity in that three successive Cup Finals were won with three different left wingers.

The long gap from 1903-28 had the occasional humorous flicker as Bob McPhail recalls. "I had just joined Rangers from Airdrie with whom I had won a medal in 1924. On training days Jock Buchanan, who had also won a medal with Morton in 1922, would take his watch chain from his suit (we dressed very formally then) and say, "Have you seen this Bob? Oh yes, of course, you have one. Where's yours Alan?" (This to Morton) and then, "Have you got yours with you Davie?" (this to Meiklejohn). I can tell you that neither of them appreciated the joke too much."

The late 1930s were a fallow period and of course the war put paid to the Scottish Cup until 1947 and it is Rangers success the following year, again the first of three on the trot, that brings in the mail. The 1948 final against Morton set up a record aggregate attendance for the two matches although interestingly enough the first final, highly unusually then, went to extra time. The reason was that there was an export drive on at the time and the government was anxious to cut down on midweek games which might cause factory and mining absenteeism. In this match Billy Williamson began his habit of popping up for an odd game in the first team and scoring a vital goal, the winner here as it happened. George Young had two from the spot the following year against Clyde and the 1950 final against East Fife was over almost before it had started.

Sometimes one single event catches the imagination in a final and in Coronation Year, 1953, it was the heroics of George Niven who, carried off with a bad head wound, returned to keep goal and earn a 1-1 draw against a fine Aberdeen side and then success in the replay. In the best Biblical fashion there then followed seven lean years before a welcome win against Kilmarnock in 1960 and another treble from 1962-64. In the first of these, good displays for St Mirren by George McLean and Thorolf Beck would eventually see both men land at Ibrox while the next two finals were noteworthy for the quality of football displayed. Often Scottish Cup Finals are grim, nerve-ridden affairs but the display against Celtic in the 1963 replay was one of the most marked ascendancy in any match between the two sides. And by common consent the 3-1 win against Dundee in 1964 was one of the best finals of all time for despite the apparently emphatic scoreline the result was doubtful until the last five minutes.

We now enter a strange period. It is beyond dispute that Celtic dominated league football from 1966-74 and yet in this time Rangers record in the Cup was good and indeed it was very useful against Celtic themselves. In 1966 came the famous 1-0 replay win when Kai Johanson's goal became perhaps the most famous

Player manager Jock Wallace, then of Berwick Rangers, giant killers and his only local player, Alan Ainslie a painter, hear the news of the Cup luck for the second round in January 1967

goal scored by a foreign player in Old Firm matches. Celtic were the winners in 1969 and 1971, the latter match memorable for the totally unexpected appearance of Jim Denny in the replay – for it is not given to many to make their debut in a Scottish Cup Final.

Rangers had their revenge in 1973, all the more gratifying since it was the club's Centenary Year and no one who was there will ever forget Tom Forsyth's sclaffed six-incher! The next win, in 1976 against Hearts is remembered for Derek Johnstone's unique feat in scoring before the official kick-off time and Rangers won looking round. The 1978 Final seems to have made most impression by the Aberdeen goal, a shot from Ritchie going up vertically and dropping behind Peter McCloy who was actually swinging on the crossbar at the time! As Rangers were two up and there was about a minute to go the goal could be enjoyed as a curiosity rather than as a source of concern. In 1979 it required three games to dispose of Hibernian and the first two matches, no-scoring draws, were so dreadful that they paved the way for the decision on the day which is now a basic part of Scottish Cup Finals. That was slightly in the future and the 1981 Dundee United tie required a replay although it would not have done had Ian Redford converted a last-minute penalty.

It would be 11 years before Rangers lifted the trophy again and therefore the win against Airdrieonians was very welcome, even if what the form book dictated. Having rediscovered how to win the old pot Rangers did it again against Aberdeen and in so doing became the first team to win it away from Hampden since 1924, as the game was played at Parkhead because of the refurbishment of the south side ground.

There are few letters about Rangers in the Cup pre-1914. This betokens the dying off of football watchers of that period and also the fact that Rangers did not find the Scottish Cup a happy competition at that period with only three wins before 1914. There might well have been a fourth but for the withholding of the Cup in season 1908-09 following the Hampden Riot. This was a curiosity in Scottish football since both sets of supporters joined forces to attack the police, having been incensed at the failure to play extra time, which did not happen in those days until the third match. Trouble was large-scale, there was much damage done but only one arrest. The detained man could fairly claim to have been the unluckiest spectator in the history of Scottish football!

BRIDGETON CROSS (Glasgow) **Please give the year when there was a break-in at Shawfield Park when Clyde and Rangers were playing a Scottish Cup tie. Were Rangers punished by being expelled from the competition?**

This was a second-round tie in 1912. Play was stopped with fifteen minutes to go when Clyde were leading 3-1. There was no direct disciplinary action involved as the Rangers Board took a unanimous decision to withdraw from the competition.

WEE ECK (Saltcoats) **What was Rangers best-ever performance in the FA Cup and why did they stop competing?**

In season 1886-87 they got to the semi-final where they were beaten 3-1 by Aston Villa at Crewe. Shortly afterwards the SFA, concerned at the disruption of Scottish fixtures, forbade clubs in its membership to enter competitions which were not under their direct control.

KINGSWAY (Glasgow) **Please give the Old Firm teams in the Scottish Cup Final of 1966 and the time of Kaj Johansen's winner in the replay.**

Teams in the 0-0 draw on the Saturday were, RANGERS, Ritchie, Johansen, Provan, Greig, McKinnon, Millar, Henderson, Watson, Forrest, Johnston, Wilson.

CELTIC, Simpson, Craig, Gemmell, Murdoch, McNeill, Clark, Johnstone, McBride, Chalmers, Auld, Hughes.

In the replay there was only one change, George McLean coming in at number 9 for Rangers in place of Jim Forrest. Johansen's winner came after 70 minutes.

BRIAR BANK (Milton of Campsie) **Scorers and crowd please at a Scottish Cup tie in the early 1960s when Rangers beat Airdrieonians 5-0 at Ibrox.**

Nearest I can find is the first-round tie of February 5, 1966 when Rangers won 5-1 (note the score). For Rangers George McLean (3), Wilson and Willie Johnston scored and in addition McLean missed a penalty. Will have the other details for you soon.

CESSNOCK BILL (Glasgow) Please give details, including the crowd of a Scottish Cup replay in which Rangers beat Aberdeen 5-1 in the early 1960s.

This was a third round replay of February 21, 1962 when the teams were, RANGERS, Ritchie, Shearer, Caldow, Davis, Baillie, Baxter, Henderson, McMillan, Millar, Brand, Wilson. ABERDEEN, Ogston, Bennet, Hogg, Brownlee, Kinnell, Fraser, Ewen, Little, Cummings, Cooke, Mulhall.

In Rangers nap-hand McMillan, Millar (2), Wilson and Brand scored for Rangers with Cummings replying for Aberdeen before a crowd of 57,000.

SAM (Fallin) Can you tell me the teams and score in the Scottish Cup Final of 1935?

Rangers won this by 2-1 when the following teams turned out, RANGERS, Dawson, Gray, McDonald, Kennedy, Simpson, Brown, Main, Venters, Smith, McPhail, Gillick.

HAMILTON ACADEMICALS, Morgan, Wallace, Bulloch, Cox, McStay, Murray, King, McLaren, Wilson, Harrison, Reid.

BIG BOOT (Linthouse) At the time of writing, 1986, which Rangers player has scored the most goals in Scottish Cup Finals?

Derek Johnstone, with five goals is out in front.

TEN MEN (Lennoxtown) Can you trace a Scottish Cup Final in which Rangers played more than half the match with ten men?

George Niven missed a large part of the first half against Aberdeen in 1953 (Rangers eventually winning after a replay) but against Morton in 1922 Andy Cunningham was taken off with a broken jaw after only 25 minutes. Morton won this one 1-0.

MITT (Duke Street) Please give details of the 1993 Scottish Cup win of Rangers over Aberdeen. Was Neil Murray the first-

ever Rangers player to score in a Scottish Cup Final at Parkhead?

Rangers beat Aberdeen 2-1 before a crowd of 50,715 spectators. Teams were, RANGERS, Goram, McCall, Robertson, Gough, McPherson, Brown, Murray, Ferguson, Durrant, Hateley, Huistra.

ABERDEEN, Snelders, McKimmie, Wright, Grant, Irvine, McLeish, Richardson, Mason, Booth, Shearer, Paataleinen.

In scoring the opening Rangers goal Neil Murray was not the first Rangers player to score in a Scottish Cup Final at Parkhead. Other scorers were Hateley for Rangers and Richardson for Aberdeen. Rangers first goal in a Scottish Cup final at Parkhead had been scored as far back as season 1902-03 when A Mackie scored the first of two goals in a 2-0 win over Hearts after two drawn matches.

MARYMASS (Irvine) In 1948 Billy Williamson of Rangers won a Scottish Cup medal having played only in the final replay. Is he the only player to have done this?

No. In 1938 John Harvey of Hearts was temporarily transferred to East Fife and assisted them to beat Kilmarnock 4-2 after extra time. He took the place of Herd, the left half, injured on the Saturday.

ROSEWEIR (East Kilbride) Please give the names of the substitutes used by Rangers in their Scottish Cup finals with Aberdeen in 1978 and Hibernian (second replay)in 1979.

The substitutes used were Watson against Aberdeen and Smith and Miller against Hibernian.

CHAPTER TWENTY-THREE

The Ulster Connection, Players from Ireland

It is the oldest of sayings that "if you become a teacher, by your pupils you'll be taught" and often in the search for an answer one discovers facts that are new and interesting.

It is not surprising that Rangers with a strong Ulster connection should have relied heavily from time to time on players from that part of the world. What is surprising is that it started comparatively late with Alec Craig, a full-back, being the first Rangers player to be capped for Ireland (as it then was) in the early years of this century.

It was after the First World War that Ulster men began to figure seriously in the Rangers team planning. Throughout the 1920s there was an all-Irish partnership at full back between Bert Manderson and Billy McCandless. Both would have distinguished careers in football when their playing days had ended. The following decade saw the trend continue. In defence there was the stuffy Bob Hamilton and the other, Bob, McDonald. Up front there was the ill-fated Sam English and that most elegant of inside-forwards Alec Stevenson who got his first three caps with Rangers and fourteen years later was still picking them up with Everton in 1948.

The rate slowed up after the return of peacetime football in 1945 and for many years Billy Simpson was the only player from the other side of the water to make much of an impression at Ibrox, gaining all his twelve caps while a Rangers player. Just when it seemed that a long-lasting link had been broken two more Northern Ireland players arrived.

John McClelland gained almost all his caps with Rangers while the case of Jimmy Nicholl was almost exactly the opposite. His international days were drawing to a close when he became a Ranger but he still managed to add three to his list of international honours while at Ibrox. In recent years such signings from Ulster as Philip Knell and John Morrow have shown promise without managing to make the final breakthrough but it would be a rash judgement to say that Ulster has finally served its purpose as a recruiting ground.

RANGERS AND ULSTER PLAYERS

PLAYFAIR (Riddrie) When Billy Simpson was transferred to Rangers was the fee a record at that time for the Ibrox club?
Rangers paid their highest fee to that date when they signed the Linfield striker in October 1950.

MAGIC SPONGE (Strathbungo) When did Bert Manderson become trainer of Queen's Park?
He took up this post at Hampden in the close season of 1928.

HODDAK (Glasgow) Did Bert Manderson give up football after leaving Rangers or did he continue as a player? Would he ever have played with Herbert Lock while at Ibrox?
Bert Manderson left Rangers in 1927 and went to England where he had a season with Bradford Park Avenue before becoming trainer with Queen's Park. He would have played at least one full season, namely 1919-20 with Herbert Lock as his goalkeeper at Ibrox.

NIGHT PORTER (Glasgow) How long was Billy McCandless with Rangers and how many League games did he play?
He was ten seasons at Ibrox and in all played 265 matches of which only 4 were in the last two seasons.

A. C. (Glasgow) Did Rangers ever play a team called Ulster in Toronto?

This match was the first of the tour of 1930 to Canada when Rangers were hard-pressed in winning 4-3. This was the first and most difficult of their 14 consecutive wins on this trip.

LOBBY DOSSER (Uddingston) Who is the last player to date from Northern Ireland who has held down a regular place in the Rangers first team?

There would really be nothing in it between John McClelland and Jimmy Nicholl.

SHAME TO TAKE IT (Mosspark) I say that John Morrow who was released by Rangers in 1994 never played for their league side.

Hope you have no money on it. I myself saw John Morrow play very well against St Johnstone in a match at McDiarmid Park round about 1992. You are however correct in thinking that the player comes from Northern Ireland.

TRUE TO THE LAST (Clydebank) Were Rangers invited to play in Belfast in a testimonial match for northern Ireland's ex-manager Billy Bingham and did they decline?

I gather the idea was mooted but the authorities in Northern Ireland feared there might be a security risk involved.

RANGERS AND ROMAN CATHOLICS

MICHAEL F. (Coventry) I say that as of now, 1970, Rangers have not had a Catholic in their first team.

That is not the case. Not long before the First World War Willie Kivlichan (who later went to Celtic) and Colin Mainds both appeared on several occasions for the Rangers league side.

A. H. (Dumfries) When did Willie Kivlichan leave Rangers to play for Celtic?

He had the one season with Rangers in 1906-07. He had 11 league games and became a Celtic player in May 1907. He was, as you suggest a doctor and I can think of three other players at Ibrox who became medicos, Doctors Paterson, Marshall and Little.

CORONA (Shawlands) Who was the Rangers manager when Maurice Johnston was signed from a French club?

Graeme Souness was in charge at Ibrox when Maurice Johnston became a Rangers player.

Opposite
Graeme Souness with signing Maurice Johnston

CHAPTER TWENTY-FOUR

Taking The Shilling – the Road from Hampden to Ibrox

The movement of Queen's Park players to Ibrox became such a well-established one in Scottish football that it is odd to think that in the very early days there was a fair traffic in the opposite direction with such stars as the great goalkeeper George Gillespie moving to Queen's Park from Rangers. This Hampden-Ibrox route was well established before 1914 with R S McColl, one of the greatest ever Scottish centre-forwards joining up at Ibrox before going on to make a fortune from sweets, hence his nickname, "Toffee Bob".

In the last years before 1914 the club would acquire a future chairman from Queen's Park in the shape of the elegant forward, James Bowie.

In 1920 Alan Morton arrived from the Amateurs, perhaps the greatest-ever such signing but there was no particular rush to follow him through the 1920s when Queens succeeded in holding on to most of their players. There was the occasional move in the 1930s, Willie Nicholson did well enough to win a Scottish Cup medal at Ibrox and great consternation was caused when T H Soutar, "Tosie", signed in 1935 as he was a lawyer and lawyers simply did not turn professional. He had torn Rangers defence apart in a 3-3 draw at Ibrox and had been signed on the strength of it although he was basically a rugby player.

It was after 1945 that there was a floodtide from Hampden to Ibrox. Indeed, in the middle 1950s and given just a couple of years licence either side, it would almost have been possible to field a first-team Rangers side who had begun their football careers at Hampden. Such a side would have included Bobby Brown in goal, Johnny Little and Sammy Cox at full-back, Ian McColl and John Valentine in the half-back line and Derek Grierson and Max Murray up front. On the curiosity side, Rangers signed a Queen's Park inside-forward in 1946 who spent almost all his time at Ibrox keeping goal for the reserves!

The fact that an amateur could negotiate his own transfer fee made such a move very attractive but the flow slackened as Queen's Park slid towards the lower reaches of Scottish football. There was still the odd movement but Derek Parlane and Alistair Scott could count themselves among the last of the Mohicans. Now if Willie Woodburn had signed for Queen's Park instead of simply playing a couple of trials for them what a side that would have made!

RANGERS AND QUEEN'S PARK QUESTIONS

LYCEUM BAR (Govan) Did Queen's Park once score seven goals in league football in a season against Rangers but fail to win a match?

They did this over two games in season 1956-57 drawing 3-3 at Ibrox and then going down 6-4 in a high-scoring match at Hampden.

VETERAN VENDOR (Queen Street) What was the maximum number of ex-Queen's Park players in a Rangers team and was this equalled or exceeded by any other Scottish team?

Around 1950 there were occasions when Rangers played four ex-Queen's Park players in their side, Brown, Cox, McColl and Liddell. Curiously enough at this very same time Morton also fielded four men, Mitchell, Whigham, Alexander and Farquhar who had had a Hampden connection.

BUTTERY (Glasgow) Did Derek Grierson or Max Murray sign first for Rangers from Queen's Park and did either or both of them win a Scottish Cup medal?

Derek Grierson was at Ibrox about five years ahead of Max Murray who became a Ranger in 1955-56. Max Murray has no Scottish Cup medals but Derek Grierson won one with Rangers and then another with Falkirk later on.

CHAPTER TWENTY-FIVE

The Two World Wars

There are many more questions about the Second World War than the First. This is not merely a reflection of the lapse of time but also a recognition that Rangers were much more successful during the second conflict.

The First World War saw football in a strange twilight zone. On the one hand the League continued, co-inciding with a great run of form by Celtic. Only in the last season of the war, 1917-18, did Rangers take the championship. Towards the end too, clubs such as Dundee and Aberdeen had dropped out temporarily but the official competition continued. It is odd that in those circumstances the Scottish Cup should not have been carried on as well but it was put into cold storage which of course goes a fair way to account for the 25 year gap between Rangers successes of 1903 and 1928.

It was hard to raise a team in the war years. Rangers were hauled before the Scottish League for fielding only nine men in a match at Brockville against Falkirk in 1915. On another occasion they generously allowed Partick Thistle to field a substitute in a match at Firhill but were rebuked again for this over-lax interpretation of the rules.

When war came again in 1939 William Struth was determined to do the best he could for his club and to compete wholeheartedly. His job was to field the best side he could and in this he was helped by the fact that many of his side were in their late twenties and therefore not eligible for call-up right away. Indeed of the recognised Ibrox first-team only Willie Thornton and Davie Kinnear were to be called up and during the war the Rangers side remained astonishingly consistent. A serviceman coming home on leave in 1944 would have recognised eight or nine of the side from 1939.

Because of this Rangers seldom needed to employ guest players, at any rate on a short-term basis. Players such as the gifted Willie McIntosh from St Johnstone who took Thornton's place and the old favourite, Torry Gillick, spent so long at Ibrox that they were virtually staff players and of course Gillick rejoined Rangers at the end of the war.

There was the odd star appearance. Stanley Matthews helped win a Charity Cup Final in 1941 and George Hamilton of Aberdeen played occasionally, but for the most part the club was represented by the tried and trusted. Only Hibernian used wartime football as well, with the result that when peacetime football resumed in 1946 they were the major challengers to Rangers for the next five years.

Rangers totally dominated those competitions which were played, winning the Regional League championship in 1940 and the Southern League championship in the following six years. They won the Southern League Cup four times out of six starts and would have been favourites to make that five had not Jerry Dawson broken a leg during a League Cup Final. They were quick to field a second eleven in 1941 in the newly-formed North-Eastern League and this gave what was a reserve team the opportunity to play against first-eleven strength sides such as Aberdeen, Raith Rovers and East Fife.

It would be fair to say that only one outstanding player came through during the war, but he was truly outstanding. This was the gigantic George Young who came to Ibrox in 1941 and took over from Willie Woodburn at centre-half before releasing that position to Woodburn when he himself moved to right-back.

A question which is forever cropping up is whether the 8-1 defeat of Celtic on January 1, 1943 is a record. The answer is that it is the highest score only, but not an official match since several of the strongest Scottish clubs were not members of the Southern League. Rangers supporters can take comfort in the fact that had it been official, then the 8-1 defeat by Hibernian at Easter Road in September 1941 would also have to be counted. The highly successful wartime period was finished off by taking the Victory Cup in 1946, something that the earlier side of 1919 had not been able to manage. Perhaps the lasting memory of the Second World War, and the reason for the large number of letters on the subject, is that during this period Rangers achieved almost total domination over Celtic whose whole attitude to the wartime game was listless and apathetic. They, like Rangers, had the great bulk of their fine 1938 side available throughout the war but allowed several of their best-known players to drift away and Rangers were to take full advantage of this carelessness.

WARTIME FOOTBALL

BLUE NOSE (Dalmuir) Did Les McDowall of Manchester City and Stanley Matthews of Stoke City and Blackpool ever play for Rangers during the Second World War?

Leslie McDowall had three first-team games for Rangers in the Southern League in season 1941-42. Stanley Matthews had a Southern League match against Morton in 1940 and he was in the side which won the Glasgow Charity Cup in May 1941 by defeating Partick Thistle 3-0 at Hampden.

TAYSIDER (Knightswood) What was the Dundee United side that played against Rangers in the first of the wartime finals?

At Hampden in May 1940 this team lost 1-0 to Rangers: Thomson, Miller, Dunsmore, Baxter, Littlejohn, Robertson, Glen, Gardiner, Milne, Adamson, Fraser.

SPORTS FAN (Glasgow) How many goals did Rangers score during their membership of the Southern League?

In the six seasons in which they were members (1940-41 till

1945-46) Rangers in all Southern League matches scored a total of 513 league goals.

N. D. P. (Govan) Did George Hamilton of Aberdeen and Scotland ever turn out for Rangers?

Not in officially recognised league matches but he did play in three Southern League matches and two Glasgow Cup ties in season 1940-41.

Calling DISPATCH (Glasgow)

The match in which Stanley Matthews played against Morton took place in March 1940 at Ibrox when the Rangers side read, Dawson, Gray, Shaw, McKillop, Woodburn, Brown, Matthews, Duncanson, Thornton, Venters, McNee.

MILTONBANK (Glasgow) I am especially interested in the North-Eastern League in which Rangers ran a side during the Second World War. Could you give me a typical Rangers North-Eastern League side of 1942-43?

This side turned out on several occasions about that time: Jenkins, Nimmo, Lindsay, Bolt, Woodburn, Marshall, McKinnon, Cargill, Smith, Venters, McCormack. Others who played in that season were Joe Craven at full-back and Davie Kinnear and Alec Beattie at outside left.

FOND MEMORY (Linthouse) One of the best Rangers centre-forwards I ever saw was Willie McIntosh. Can you tell me anything about him?

The most unusual thing about him is that he was never a signed Rangers player. He signed for St Johnstone just before the war in 1939 from Petershill. When St Johnstone closed down in 1940 he moved to Rangers on a wartime basis and played very successfully for about three seasons. Later in the war he played for Third Lanark before returning to St Johnstone at the end of hostilities. I quite agree with your assessment of the player.

WELLPARK (Glasgow) Can you trace Rangers beating Celtic five times in a season sometime in the 1940s?

In season 1945-46 the two sides met six times, Rangers winning five and the other match being drawn.

THE DUKE (Bellshill) What was the score in a friendly match

at Ibrox between Rangers and Newcastle United right at the end of the Second World War?

This match was played on Tuesday September 25, 1945 and Rangers won 3-2. Scorers for Rangers were Williamson (2), and Duncanson with Milburn and Wayman replying for United. George Young also missed a penalty for Rangers.

CONUNDRUM (Partick) How does it come about that Rangers played Airdrie and Dumbarton during the war when they were not First Division clubs?

This came about because after the fall of France in 1940 football was organised on regional lines. Clubs such as Aberdeen, Dundee, Raith Rovers and St Johnstone dropped out for the time being and so too did Kilmarnock and Ayr United. In their places came such clubs as the two you mention and also Queen's Park who had in fact been relegated in 1939.

CHAPTER TWENTY-SIX

The League Cup

The one thing that can be said with certainty is that no Rangers fan ever writes in to demand the result of the 1957 League Cup final. They are all for drawing a decent veil over the 7-1 defeat by Celtic.

It has been a strange competition for Rangers. Winners twice in the first three competitions it was then 12 years before their next success. There followed a good spell in the early 1960s and then an in-and-out period before Rangers began to make a habit of annexing this trophy in the middle 1980s.

The first success in 1946-47 against Aberdeen was very welcome since the result had gone against Rangers with the same opponents the previous season. This time astonishingly Aberdeen chose to play against driving rain and a fierce wind and the game was effectively over at half-time with Rangers three ahead. This was not the first time that weather had played a key role. In a wartime League Cup Final of 1943 when the weather was so abysmal that several players collapsed with exhaustion a Rangers-Falkirk match nevertheless went ahead. Interestingly, because weather was a wartime secret the match had to go on although by the time the Germans found out it was a filthy day in Glasgow it is hard to see what they could have done with the information.

What games especially stand out? The 1963 win over Morton by 5-0 because Morton had electrified Scottish football by doing so well as a Second Division club in reaching the final and because

Four Hibernian players cannot prevent Ally McCoist getting in the overhead kick which brought the winning goal in the League Cup for Rangers at Parkhead in October 1993

Derek Johnstone slips his markers, Billy McNeill and Jim Craig to head the goal that won the League Cup for Rangers at Hampden in October 1970

the cousins partnership of Alex Willoughby and Jim Forrest was at the height of its efficiency. There are still letters on the three consecutive Old Firm finals of 1964 to 1966 of which Rangers won the first and then came the Old Firm final of 1970. The 1-0 win, with the young Derek Johnstone scoring, was not only priceless in that the trophy was won, but an indication that perhaps the first cracks were appearing in the great Celtic side which had won the European Cup.

Between 1975 and 1986 there were five more meetings with never more than a goal between the sides but Rangers took the cup on all but one occasion. None of these were particularly memorable games except for the McCoist hat-trick which brought a 3-2 win in 1982.

The connoisseurs were much more delighted with the three successive marvellous matches with Aberdeen which began in 1987. The first of them, which Rangers won on penalty kicks after a 3-3 extra time draw was widely compared with the immortal Real Madrid v Eintracht Frankfurt match, and if the football did not quite perhaps reach that rarified level it was a more exciting match because it was that much more even. A curious fact is that in all the years of the League Cup's being played under conventional rules neither Rangers nor Celtic ever lost in a final replay.

LEAGUE CUP QUESTIONS

COME AGAIN (Glasgow) Is Jim Forrest the only Rangers player to have scored four goals in a major cup final?
Yes, Jim hit four goals in Rangers 5-0 win over Morton in the League Cup final of season 1963-64.
QUIZ KING (Glasgow) Did Derek Johnstone win a League Cup medal against Celtic in 1975-76 in the inside-left position and does this give him major medals in five different positions?
He did and it does, the other positions in four Scottish Cup finals being No 9, No 5, No 7 and No 4.

HOLD IT UP (Busby) Please give details of Rangers matches from the quarter-finals on when they won the League Cup in 1984-85.

In a one-off quarter-final they beat Cowdenbeath 3-1 at Central Park. Over a two-legged semi-final they beat Meadowbank Thistle 4-0 at Ibrox and drew 1-1 at Tynecastle (the match being played there for security reasons). In the final Rangers beat Dundee United 1-0.

TWEED (Grangemouth) What is the greatest number of penalty kicks awarded in a League Cup Final?

Three in the Old Firm League Cup final of 1983-84 which Rangers won 3-2. Ally McCoist scored two from the spot for Rangers and Mark Reid tucked one away for Celtic.

CHAPTER TWENTY-SEVEN

The English in Competition

In this section, like the proverbial small boy, Rangers have saved the best bit for last with their recent fine performances against Leeds United in Europe. There had been meetings in competition with English clubs before, Rangers defeating Everton in the British League Cup of 1902 before falling in the final to Celtic. This was a trophy taken seriously as it was played to raise money for the Ibrox Disaster Fund and the participants were Sunderland and Everton, champions and runners-up of the Football League and Rangers and Celtic who held similar positions in Scotland.

The next major Anglo-Scottish competition, the Exhibition Tournament of 1938 brought Rangers and Everton together again and a loss on their own Ibrox was disappointing for Rangers even if with Torry Gillick and Alex Stevenson on the Everton side it could have been argued that it is not lost what a friend gets.

Rangers were no more successful in the Coronation Cup of 1953, losing to Manchester United at Hampden. But by now European competitive football was knocking at the door and Rangers first performance against English opposition at this level was outstanding. Wolverhampton Wanderers were still a power in the land in 1961 – only a few years before they had taken on and humbled the best sides in Europe at Molyneaux Park, including the famous Hungarians of Honved. They found Rangers too hot for them however and the Ibrox side in winning 2-0 at home gave themselves an effective cushion, which a marvellous display by Billy Ritchie in goal extended into a 0-0 draw on the trip south.

Two years later, again in the European Cup Winners competition, a visit to London went markedly less well. Rangers scored twice at White Hart Lane and that was certainly not unsatisfactory, but the defence conceded goals like a drunken sailor spending money on shore leave. No answer was found to Spurs ploy of inswinging corner kicks and five goals were lost. The second leg at Ibrox was postponed because of industrial fog (almost the last time this would happen) and when the match went ahead Rangers again scored twice but at the other end the defence was breached three times. Hopes were high when Rangers took on Newcastle United at Ibrox in the first leg of the Fairs Cities Cup semi-final in 1969. But when the Geordie keeper McFaul saved an Andy Penman penalty, a 0-0 draw was not good enough for St James's Park where United won 2-0 in a match marred by crowd trouble.

There then followed a long gap until in the early 1980s Chesterfield were the improbable opponents in an improbable competition, the Anglo-Scottish Cup. The result, a whacking 3-0 win for Chesterfield, and a loss for aggregate of 4-1 was even more improbable and no, I don't get too many requests about line-ups and scorers at Saltergate.

So to the great redemption. There were widespread predictions of woe when Rangers came out of the hat against Leeds United in the European Cup competition of 1993-94. Our game was not held in esteem down south. Chesterfield hadn't helped nor had Celtic's feeble capitulation to Burnley in the same competition. The predictions of woe redoubled as Gary McAllister scored a first-minute goal at Ibrox in what was literally total silence. Nothing in recent years has been more impressive than the manner in which Rangers clawed themselves back into the game. At the end they led by 2-1 and I had seen enough to go the following morning to place a bet on their winning not only the tie but the second leg at Leeds. I knew they had the legs of the Yorkshiremen and in the event Hateley and McCoist destroyed them while Goram kept them out, Cantona and all. It was a result which gave the game in the north a tremendous boost and Rangers earned the gratitude of the thinking Scottish game.

ENGLISH CLUBS
IN COMPETITIVE MATCHES

CRUSADER (Falkirk) When Rangers beat Wolverhampton Wanderers at Ibrox by 2-0 in the European Cup Winners tournament in 1961 did they play with ten men? How many Scots were in the Wolverhampton side and what was the crowd?

This match, watched by 80,000 spectators was played on March 29, 1961. Harold Davis was injured after only ten minutes and limped on the right-wing for the rest of the match. Goalkeeper Malcolm Finlayson was the only Scot in the Wolves line-up in this match.

GOVAN DEPOT (Glasgow) When Rangers met Tottenham Hotspur in the Cup Winners Cup were Danny Blanchflower, John White and Jimmy Greaves in the Tottenham side?

All three players you name took part in both games. You are right in saying that the return leg at Ibrox, which Spurs won 3-2 had been put back for almost a week because of heavy fog on the original night.

BESTEVER (Royston) Was the Rangers team which beat Leeds United home and away in the Europoean Cup unchanged in both matches? What were the respective attendances and did Cantona score for Leeds United ?

Rangers made one change for the second match at Elland Road, Dale Gordon coming in for Trevor Steven. The crowds were 44,000 at Ibrox and 25,118 at Elland Road. Cantona scored for Leeds after Hateley and McCoist had given Rangers a 2-0 lead.

CHAPTER TWENTY-EIGHT

Rangers Sports

For many years the highlight of the Scottish athletic calendar was the Rangers Sports, traditionally held on the first Saturday in August. This reflected the interest of William Struth who had started his sporting career as a "ped", a professional runner. In his time as manager he attracted the very best athletes in world competition, very often persuading them to make the detour north on their way to the A A A Championships in London or even as in 1948 en route to the Olympic Games at Wembley.

Some of the finest athletes of all time appeared at the Ibrox Sports. The great Finnish runner Paavo Nurmi set up a record for the rather unusual distance of four miles and before that W Halswell, a winner in the London Olympics of 1908 established a 440 yards record in that same year. In 1913 the great English sprinter, W R Applegarth, bettered ten seconds for the hundred yards.

Between the wars the stars continued to shine. The outstanding little miler Sydney Wooderson, who was to get as near the four-minute mile as anyone before 1939, appeared frequently. So too did the dashing New Zealand miler, Jack Lovelock and the Scots-descended hurdler, Donald Findlay who had the distinction of representing his country at the London Olympics of 1948 while bearing the exalted rank of Group Captain in the Royal Air Force.

The great Scots high jumper, Alan Paterson recorded a personal best in 1947 when he jumped 6' 7.5" and had he been able to repeat this at Wembley the following year he would have won the first gold medal for Scotland since Eric Liddell in 1924 at Paris.

The sports were not all about the high and mighty of course. There were the handicap events with runners from Bellahouston Harriers, from Garscube, from Victoria Park, from Springburn and from Shettleston, all very dear to Bill Struth's heart. There were the handicap distance races with the less talented racers strung out almost out of sight. There were the cycle sprints and deil-tak'-the-hindmost races.

Above all, there were the five-a-sides and in all honesty probably as much as half the crowd had come to see them. This fascinating abbreviated game, with its long lethargic periods punctuated by bursts of frenzied activitiy, its bizarre method of settling games by corners so that flag kicks were heralded almost as loudly as goals, could be depended upon to stir the crowd to a frenzy and was a sign that the start of the real season was only a week away.

The sports did not long survive the Second World War and there were essentially two main reasons for this. The A A A moved their own championship meeting to the first Saturday in August and it became ever harder to attract top-flight athletes to compete on that Saturday in direct opposition. Struth was not interested in second-best in athletics any more than in football. To add to this by the early 1950s he was visibly failing and those who came after him had begun to regard the annual meeting as something of a diversion from the more serious business. Within a few years of Struth's resignation and death the Rangers Sports had passed into history but not before they had provided splendid entertainment for the 30,000 crowds which regularly turned up to greet the stars of track and field and the imminent arrival of the new season.

SPORTS

CINDERSIFTER (Gourock) When were the Rangers sports traditionally held?

Certainly from the 1930s they were held on the first Saturday in August as the curtain-raiser to the new football season. About 1960 the AAA in England appropriated this date for their championships and it became impossible to attract athletes of sufficient standing to justify continuing the meeting.

BALLWATCHER (Busby) How many teams took part in the five-a-sides at the Rangers sports?

I remember seeing the six Glasgow clubs during the war but I have a notion that eight was the normal peacetime figure. Corners of course counted to decide the winners.

YOUNG 'UN (Dunoon) Was Bill Struth's own background in athletics?

Yes, he had been a professional runner as a young man. The demarcation between amateur and professional was very strict in those days and a professional runner, or "ped", as they were known was automatically debarred from the major athletics championships.

CHAPTER TWENTY-NINE

Showing The Flag – the Early Days

From the beginning of organised football the major Scottish sides deemed it a duty and a privilege to take the game to other regions of the world. For Rangers that meant Canada and the two successful tours of 1928 and 1930. Jerry Dawson was in no doubt that he had enjoyed the best of playing abroad. In an interview with me in the 1970s when competitive European football had become the norm he had this to say.

"We played in the palmy days of football. In the circumstances of the time we were millionaires. We paid Income Tax at the end of the year and we made with bonuses about £15 per week. We had much better tours abroad than now. We went by boat, we had time to see the country, we lived like lords and the opposition were pushovers. Now it is a very hasty flight and a really tough match."

Wise words, but even in Dawson's own time there had been signs that the cakewalks were ending. By the middle 1930s Austrian football in particular was flourishing as a 50,000 crowd could testify after it had watched Sportsklub Rapid of Vienna draw 3-3 at Ibrox in 1933. When later that summer two matches were lost on a German tour, even although there were four wins to set against this, it became clear that it was not advisable to send jaded players abroad at the end of a season to take on comparatively fresh Europeans. It would be the middle 1950s before all ideas of the taxing close-season tour in Europe would be abandoned but a combination of indifferent results on a Spanish tour and the almost-simultaneous emergence of European competition put an end to such visits with scarce an exception.

Now that we are very willing to acknowledge that over the piece Continental football is better than our own it is amusing to look back to the 1930s and reflect that caps were not awarded for matches against European countries nor was anything like our strongest side selected for such a fixture. These matches were seen as a pleasant way of rewarding the "nearly men" but basically were not treated all that seriously. We were to pay a heavy price for refusing to heed what was going on under our noses.

The relaxed tours of which Jerry Dawson spoke so eloquently made abundant sense. The long journeys fostered team spirit and there were just enough games to keep the players in a close-season standard of fitness without being the treadmill extension of the season affairs that they have become today. We will have to relearn the old truth that very often it is mental exhaustion that curtails the career of a player rather than physical debility.

Copies of photos in this book are available from:

Photo Sales Dept.
Evening Times
195 Albion Street
Glasgow G1 1QP